CW01011489

# A Climate Change Companion

## For family, school and community

David Hicks

Teaching4abetterworld

First published in UK 2016
by Teaching4abetterworld
www.teaching4abetterworld.co.uk

© 2016 David Hicks

All rights reserved. No parts of this book may be reproduced in any form without permission from the publisher except for the quotation of brief passages in reviews. The moral right of the author has been asserted.

Cover Image © Ashden Awards 2014

ISBN: 978-1544070216

If you don't write of things

    deep inside your own heart

What's the use of churning

    out so many words


    Ryokan (1758-1831)

# Acknowledgments

To Kay, who said she wanted a good story, and to colleagues who read through earlier versions of the book - Cathie, Nick, Kay and Graham, and Steve for the clarity and detail of his editing. Gratitude also goes to Lou for her on-going support, and to Matt, Jay, Holly and Ethan for their wonderful presence in my life. I also need to acknowledge the inspiration I have received from the work of Climate Outreach, Carbon Conversations and the Transition Network. I thank you all.

# Contents

Introduction: This book.................................................1

Part One: Changing the climate.............................5

   1. What do we need to know? .............................7

   2. What's energy got to do with it? ...............23

   3. What's the choice of futures? ....................39

Part Two: Telling new stories............................ 55

   4. The old story: high-carbon ........................57

   5. The new story: low-carbon ........................73

   6. Feeling the way forward.............................88

Part Three: Working for change .......................103

   7. Getting things done.................................. 105

   8. Adapting to climate change..................... 121

   9. Limiting climate change........................... 136

Part Four: A journey of hope............................153

   10. Telling family stories............................. 155

   11. Learning about sustainability................ 171

   12. Creating low-carbon community ......... 190

Postscript: After Paris .....................................204

Sources ............................................................207

*Companion:*

    A *friend* ~ always there to turn to

    An *acquaintance* ~ may give advice

    A *supporter* ~ offers encouragement

    A *guide* ~ shows you the path

    A *partner* ~ you can really rely on

    An *ally* ~ in it for the duration

    An *assistant* ~ helps with the work

    An *associate* ~ follows a similar path

    A *comrade* ~ committed to the same values

# This book

'Not another book on climate change?' a friend said to me. I wasn't sure at the time whether she was referring to my own interest in this or the many other books written about the subject over the last twenty years. Certainly, there are a lot of useful books and websites for those who want to know more. However, it's also true that these are frequently written for or by experts and others who presume a level of knowledge the reader may not have or offer more information than one actually wants. This could be one reason why potential readers seem to avoid such a field of concern.

This book has a different intent, which is to offer something that is clear, informative, encouraging, practical and inspiring for the general reader. It is not intended as an academic book but aimed, in particular, at members of the public, concerned citizens, parents, educators, students and others who would like to gain a basic understanding and initial grasp of climate change and its significance for themselves, their families, schools and communities. In doing this the book offers responses to a number of vital questions. These include:

- ✓ What exactly is climate change?
- ✓ Why should it matter to me?
- ✓ Why is it important to my family's future?
- ✓ What are people doing about it already?
- ✓ What are the sorts of things I can do?

It draws together various interrelated threads which help set climate change in its wider cultural context. It explores the nature of people's hopes and fears about this issue and shows how our historical use of fossil fuels - coal, oil and gas - has brought great wealth and comfort to society but also increasing hazards and danger. Nearly half a century of scientific research shows quite clearly that the burning of fossil fuels results in the release of gases which lead to global warming and consequently climate change. What is also widely understood is that we must now rapidly shift to renewable forms of energy - wind, solar and water - which do not contribute to global warming. Such technologies are clean, green and safer for us, our children and grandchildren. Sometimes in history societies have realised they need to make a major shift of direction in order to survive and prosper. Many people believe we are now facing just such a dilemma. We can continue with 'business as usual' which will lead to increasingly difficult weather extremes and hazards or take up the challenge of helping to create with others a more safe, healthy and sustainable future.

The arrangement of this book is as follows. Part 1: 'Changing the Climate' looks at why one needs to understand something about climate change, how this is directly related to the historical and present day use of fossil fuels and how, as a result, we are faced with a critical choice of futures. Part 2: 'Telling New Stories' explores our emotional responses to such matters, the story that societies tell themselves about high-carbon living and a new story that highlights a low-carbon alternative. Part 3: 'Working for Change' emphasises the importance of acting together to help create a safer future, illustrating this with case studies on both how to adapt to climate change and how one can help lessen its impact. Part 4: 'A Journey of Hope' considers how this transition can begin in the home, at school and in the local community.

Often readers know little about an author beyond a brief biographical note but I think it appropriate to know something of the writer's personal story - the experiences which led to this place and from which the concerns of a book unfold. What I immediately recall, as a young teacher in the 1970s, was watching a TV documentary entitled, 'Due to lack of interest, tomorrow has been cancelled'. This examined a range of environmental issues and their likely impact on the future of society. As a young parent, I remember thinking that the future was not going to be cancelled as far as I was concerned. It was the beginning of my wanting to look ahead to check what might be coming towards us, locally, nationally or even globally, that we might need to be prepared for. As I worked in education this became part of my on-going practice with students. Which issues are likely to have the biggest impact on our future, positive or negative, and if the latter what needs to be done to help change this?

As a writer and educator, I believe one should help both adults and young people understand major issues in the world today and the things that are being done to help resolve them. I was involved for several years in a national project which explored how our local communities are always interrelated with events and issues in the wider world. I also ran a project helping young people think more critically and creatively about their futures. At the turn of the century climate change was increasingly in the news and clearly going to have a major impact on everyone's future. I began working with different groups on how they might ready themselves for the various changes this could bring. As a grandparent, I feel even more responsible for preparing parents and young people for a future that will certainly be very different from today.

This book does not discuss national and international policies relating to climate change, although clearly of importance, since there are many other sources of information available on this. What it focuses on is you, your family and community, and the major transition we are inevitably facing. May it be a useful companion on your journey.

David Hicks
Chepstow

# Part One

## Changing the climate

# 1. What do we need to know?

*Climate change is not a 'problem' waiting for 'a solution'. It is an environmental, cultural and political phenomenon which is reshaping the way we think about ourselves, our societies and humanity's place on Earth.*

- Climate scientist Mike Hulme[1]

When starting out on any new venture it's not always easy to know where to begin. There may be several possible starting points and some may be better than others. Where we start from always affects the journey we then undertake. And, when asking for directions, there's always the reply the traveller received, 'If that's where you want to get to I wouldn't start from here'. Trying to get a grip on issues relating to climate change can feel difficult. Who do I consult - journalists, politicians, scientists, educators, friends, neighbours? The results can be confusing. Everyone seems to have their own ideas, including the notion that there is no such issue in the first place. Alternatively, people may have many other pressing needs to attend to and, as one questioner said, 'Where does it all come from, this stuff about climate change? I haven't got time for it. Persuade me it really matters and I might take a look'.

## In the beginning

So where is a good place to begin? As is often the case, it's helpful to look back to see where and when a particular question or idea began to emerge in human thinking. Thus, the idea that particular gases in the atmosphere might influence the Earth's temperature has a long history, beginning in the early nineteenth century. Here are some of the key figures in that unfolding story.

It began back in the 1820s when a French physicist and mathematician, Joseph Fourier, realised there was a difference between the amount of energy reaching the Earth from the sun and the quantity reflected back into space. He reasoned there must be gases in the atmosphere that helped cause this effect. Of course, at the time, he had no idea of how important this insight was to be. Some thirty years later, in the 1850s, Irish scientist John Tyndall established that molecules of carbon dioxide, nitrous oxide and methane (later known as 'greenhouse gases') could indeed have an effect on the Earth's temperature. This was later confirmed by Svante Arrhenius, a Swedish physicist, who in the 1890s showed that changing the amount of carbon dioxide in the atmosphere could lead to changes in the surface temperature of the planet. Whilst one might think these insights pretty slim results in a century of scientific research it was partly because these scientists were ahead of their time and that the endeavours of mainstream science were elsewhere.

This important groundwork, however, was not lost but further built on some forty years later when, in 1938, British engineer Guy Callendar began to analyse meteorological statistics from around the world. What he found was a warming trend which, he argued, related to increased amounts of carbon dioxide in the atmosphere. He figured that the previously identified greenhouse gases must be responsible for this now observable trend. He also believed the cause was man-made. This proved to be the crucial breakthrough which brought together: i) the theory of carbon dioxide and the greenhouse effect; ii) the rising amount of carbon dioxide in the atmosphere; and iii) the increase in global temperatures. At the time, however, meteorologists and others were sceptical about the validity of his calculations. Then other matters intervened, the Second World War and the economic austerity of the post-war period.

But, come the 1950s, these ideas began to be taken up more widely and in particular there were attempts to verify them scientifically. In 1958 Charles Keeling, a research scientist, began to measure the amount of carbon dioxide in the atmosphere from an observatory in Hawaii to see whether this was changing. This produced the first scientific evidence that levels of carbon dioxide were increasing in the Earth's atmosphere and which continue to do so today. So, it took well over a century for developments in science to reach a point where global warming and its relationship to what became called the 'greenhouse gases' was verified.

In the 1970s, computer modelling of changes in the planet's atmosphere became possible and by the late 1980s it was accepted that this needed to include data on the atmosphere, the oceans, ice sheets, forests and land cover. Prime Minister Margaret Thatcher, with a science background, made her concerns clear in an address to the Royal Society.

> The first is the increase in the greenhouse gases—carbon dioxide, methane, and chlorofluorocarbons—which has led some to fear that we are creating a global heat trap which could lead to climatic instability. We are told that a warming effect of 1°C per decade would greatly exceed the capacity of our natural habitat to cope. Such warming could cause accelerated melting of glacial ice and a consequent increase in the sea level of several feet over the next century.[2]

The level of concern internationally was such that the Intergovernmental Panel on Climate Change (IPCC) was set up in 1988 by the World Meteorological Association and the UN Environmental Program. The task of this international body is to collect and collate research from climate scientists around the world. The IPCC is not a research body itself. With a growing wealth of scientific information from many different sources the IPCC began to assess in more and more detail the likely impacts of global warming on climate change and to formulate possible responses to these changes. In particular, their reports are aimed at governments and policy makers at all levels, those who have a responsibility to identify and implement appropriate change in the face of such hazards.

By the mid-90s climate scientists were clear that natural causes could not account for the degree of global warming they were observing. Only when possible human causes were factored in could the warming be explained - the increase in greenhouse gases came from the carbon emissions of the modern industrial world which developed and spread across the globe from the mid-century onwards. On this the science was clear and over the years computer modelling of the changing atmosphere has become increasingly complex and sophisticated so that current data can now be used to identify a range of different climate futures. Thus it's possible to input differing rates of carbon emissions - low, medium and high - to see what their different impacts on future weather might be in say ten, fifty or a hundred years time. Needless to say, the higher the carbon emissions the more difficult our weather will be.

So far, the IPCC has produced five reports on the state of climate change knowledge, the latest in November 2014. A vast amount of information has been gathered, the strength of which lies in the sheer number of scientists working internationally in the field of climate change. All such research is critically reviewed by other professionals so that the IPCC reports themselves offer a consensus, and some would say even conservative view, arrived at only after much debate and discussion. These reports need to be taken seriously and, as the latest one makes clear, there is clearly danger ahead unless we work together to avert it. They categorically stress that human activities are responsible for climate change and that this is already happening, with each of the last three decades warmer than the one before. In essence, climate change is already bringing more frequent and extreme weather across the globe and will continue to do so.

## Causes

So why does it matter if the world is warming up? Doesn't it mean we'll all be able to sunbathe on the equivalent of a tropical beach? And anyway, what makes this warming happen? Let's start with what the research tells us about why it's happening - the greenhouse gases. On the one hand, the atmosphere which surrounds our planet has just the right mix of gases to allow all sorts of life to exist, from insects and plants to animals and humans. So far this is pretty unique as astronomers have yet to identify any other planets with this particular mix. The main gases in the air are nitrogen (78%) and oxygen (21%). They don't have much effect on the climate but are vital to human, animal and plant life.

On the other hand, the difficult gases which Tyndall identified are carbon dioxide, methane and nitrous oxide. In their natural balance, they don't cause a problem. The Earth is warmed up by the sun's energy and then radiates heat back into the atmosphere, but if the levels of these gases are too high they create the 'greenhouse effect' - they trap the heat like the glass in a greenhouse, thus the term greenhouse gases. As scientists measured this warming the question they were faced with was, 'What is causing this rise in greenhouse gases? Is it natural or manmade?' Various possible causes were considered and the evidence tested again and again. In the end the answer was clear, although often not agreeable to people. It was human industrial activity that was the cause of greenhouse gases, particularly carbon dioxide. The rise of carbon emissions closely matches the rise of modern society from the Industrial Revolution onwards and the graph looks set to grow upwards even more.

Because of this, average global temperatures have grown by one degree centigrade (1C) over the last hundred years, a seemingly small amount but one which nevertheless has had a major impact on global climate. Rather than sitting around enjoying oneself on a tropical beach, the consequences of a warming climate have been much more severe. Indeed, use of the term 'warming' may have been misleading and partly responsible for that image. We should more accurately be talking about global heating. It has been calculated and largely agreed that should the average rise in global temperature exceed 2C then serious runaway climate change could occur.

So, what have we been doing without realising it to create such carbon emissions? The main cause is that over the last two-hundred years modern society has become hugely reliant on fossil fuels (oil, coal and gas) to meet many of our everyday needs. The Industrial Revolution in the eighteenth and nineteenth centuries saw a major shift from water power to the steam engine fuelled by coal. This became our main source of energy later to be succeeded by oil and gas in the twentieth century. All three provide sources of power, whether for heating, as fuels or the source of innumerable by-products, such as plastics and fertilisers. What was *not* clear from the mid-nineteenth till sometime after the mid-twentieth century was that the burning of these fossil fuels created extra greenhouse gases, leading to global warming and so to a changing climate.

## Annual Greenhouse Gas Emissions by Sector

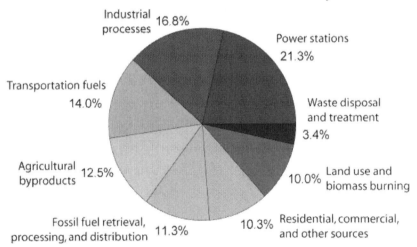

Approximate global figures for emissions from each sector of society

This is quite something to take in because it means we need to profoundly rethink the way in which we are accustomed to viewing our lives and our world. Many of the things we take for granted and which, in their time, were brilliant scientific and technological breakthroughs in the nineteenth and twentieth-centuries turn out to have a sting in their tail. If they rely on coal, oil or gas in their manufacture or use, i.e. they produce dangerous high-carbon emissions, we urgently need to be developing low-carbon alternatives. If I stop to ponder this I think about coal and oil used as a fuel, let alone the many by-products created from them, I think of modern transport, the creation of innumerable materials and gadgets, building materials and agricultural practices. Since I partake of this I have been a high-carbon emitter through much of my life without realising it.

One of the things about carbon is that it is invisible and so cannot be seen. However, once we begin to use carbon in one form or another it becomes visible, as long as we know where to look. Where in actuality in the news or online have you seen images of offshore oil rigs, coal or oil fired power stations, petrol and diesel vehicles, aircraft overhead, plastic packaging, lighting or heating left on and cleaning up oil spills on a beach? These are some of the visual indicators of our often high-carbon lifestyles.[3] I say often rather than always because the amount of carbon a country emits will depend very much on its industrial and technological history. Richer countries are high emitters and, although it might not feel like it, this includes the UK.

All sectors of society create greenhouse gases - from power stations, industry, transport and farming to homes, commerce, land use and waste disposal. The crucial task is to drastically cut the emissions arising from each of these sectors. The three chief gases involved are as follows. Carbon dioxide, mainly arising from the burning and use of fossil fuels, is the main greenhouse gas (72 percent of the total). Methane, however, arising from rice paddies, peat bogs and gestating cattle (18 percent of the total) is twenty-five times more powerful. Nitrous oxide, an industrial by-product (9 percent of the total) has some three hundred times the impact. In this book I use the term 'carbon emissions' and 'carbon footprint' to embrace all three of these main gases.

Now it could also be said that one of the causes of climate change is human appetite. Over the last forty years in the UK and other countries we have been encouraged by economists, business and advertising to consume more of nearly everything, apparently in order to feel happier and more contented. However, when asked, people tend to report that it is friends, family and work satisfaction that brings them the greatest happiness in life rather than acquisition of stuff. This ongoing stress on never-ending consumerism, the need to have more rather than enough, has and is contributing in richer countries to increasingly high carbon emissions.

The causes of climate change therefore have geophysical reasons: how the atmosphere protects the planet, but more specifically human reasons, the ways in which we and our forebears chose to live over the last two centuries. Choices which seemed the best of ideas at the time have unwittingly disturbed the balance of the atmosphere. With the knowledge we have now, comes the responsibility to find ways of working towards a low rather than a high-carbon future. So, what have been some of the consequences of inadvertently changing our climate?

## Consequences

We now know that the consequences have been many and various. Although a rise of 1C over a hundred years may seem small it has already triggered major changes. Basically, it works like this. When the atmosphere becomes warmer it is able to hold more moisture, which then makes the air more agitated. When air becomes more volatile in this way it causes more extreme weather. This warming not only applies to the atmosphere but also to the sea. When oceans get warmer the water expands and sea-levels begin to rise. This is why a changing climate is also a more difficult one. At first it was not possible for climate scientists to attribute a particular bout of extreme weather - storms, floods, drought - to climate change. However, the accuracy of climate modelling has now reached the point where it is possible to say, of particular events, it is highly likely that this is a consequence of climate change.

Newspapers tend only occasionally to report bad weather from other places in the world so we may not be particularly aware of global shifts and changes elsewhere. It is now known that the last forty years have seen many of the highest annual temperatures and increasingly frequent extreme weather conditions. One of the dilemmas in the UK is that we have an on-going history of joking about the variability in our weather, how cold or hot it was then, how wet or dry. We have been brought up to expect the weather to be variable and our experience shows this to be true. What is now being realised, however, is that our weather has begun to get more extreme as well as more variable. I remember back in the 90s thinking that we didn't used to get river flooding in the news every year and wondered whether this was anything to do with climate change. There were serious floods in the Severn Valley in 2007, west Cumbria in 2009, north Yorkshire and Tyneside in 2012, the Somerset Levels and Thames Valley in 2014. As I write in 2015 roads and bridges are destroyed in the Lake District and the city of Carlisle looks like Venice.

A newspaper headline which announced, 'No home in the UK safe from flooding,' puzzled me at first as clearly not everyone lives on the coast or near a river. What the article pointed out was that because rain is now increasingly torrential no property can be guaranteed safe in such circumstances. I am also struck by the way in which flooding rightly catches the news but how little is said about how long it takes for people to return to their homes or the trouble they have with the clean-up, loss-adjustors and insurance companies. It is not just the flooding which is a problem but the prolonged financial, emotional and mental wear and tear that often accompanies these events.

It is agreed by climate scientists that what the UK will experience is more extreme weather events: storms, heavy rain, flooding, heat-waves, drought, harsher winters; in short, our weather will become both more variable and more extreme. This is the new 'normal', something qualitatively different from the historical variability of our weather. I do not say this to be alarmist but because this is what the scientific evidence tells us. It may be inconvenient, uncomfortable and unwelcome, but both citizens and governments have a social responsibility to be prepared for these changes so that families, communities and society as a whole, know both how to adapt to these changes and to limit their impact. These events will impact on every aspect of our lives, from home and work to travel and food. As the government's Special Representative on Climate Change and former Government Chief Scientific Advisor commented, 'Climate change is not the biggest challenge of our time, it's the biggest challenge of all time'.[4]

So, what about some of the other current impacts on people and the environment around the world? At the time of writing California is just emerging from four years of drought. Two-thirds of the state experienced extreme conditions and some forty percent of the population lived with exceptional drought. Both urban and agricultural areas were affected and as the drought went on rationing and recrimination were on the increase. Did the bottled water industry deplete mountain streams in pursuit of profit? Was the intensive growing of almonds the problem since each nut needs a gallon of water to grow? State water policy was challenged as never before. At the same time, Louisiana is losing land to the sea faster than almost anywhere else in the world. Sugar-cane fields, citrus groves and backwoods have all gone under water in low-lying coastal areas near the Mississippi. It has been calculated that in some areas rising sea-level inundates the equivalent of a football pitch every hour. In part the flooding is the result of inappropriate changes in land-use and river management. It is not clear, however, whether existing plans to protect the coastline from flooding will actually work. In Australia fire-prone areas are facing more frequent and stronger bush fires. 'Uninhabitable zones' have been designated where no building is now allowed. Under a voluntary buy-back scheme the state of Victoria bought more than a hundred properties destroyed by bush fires. Whilst in some areas bush-fires are a normal part of the ecology higher temperatures and drought have exacerbated this problem.

Low-lying Pacific islands are increasingly flood-prone and their inhabitants beginning to seek refuge elsewhere; they have become climate refugees. In parts of northern Brazil there no longer appears to be a distinction between winter and summer with the weather constantly dry. The frequency of droughts has increased in southern Kenya and more cattle, the basis of people's livelihood, are dying. In Peru water and electricity supplies to urban areas are increasingly threatened because the high glaciers are melting. This affects energy supply because 70 percent of power comes from hydroelectricity. So, global heating has resulted in climate change which has led, and will continue to lead, to all sorts of changes to our normal weather patterns. Everyone is being affected, some sooner than others, but in all cases people are experiencing new or more frequent weather extremes. Headlines over the last few years include: 'Adapt to survive: superstorm Sandy has lessons for how the rest of the world will need to adapt'; 'The rise in extreme weather is a sign of things to come'; 'How a warming world is a threat to our food supplies'; 'Global warming down to 90 big firms'; 'Fighting climate change is affordable, says UN'. However, these impacts do not occur everywhere all of the time. They tend to be country and region specific and it's important to know what the new norm is likely to be in the wider area where you live.

## Decisions

Whilst the scientific community and forward thinking citizens are agreed on the hazards of climate change and the need to work towards a low-carbon future, both countries and political parties may differ in their responses. One of the tensions over trying to reach agreement on cutting carbon emissions at international conferences, such as the one in Paris 2015, is that between richer and poorer countries. The latter rightly point out it is richer industrialised countries which have caused global warming and who are therefore most responsible for climate change. Less industrialised countries know that their carbon emissions are much lower and therefore understandably feel much less responsible for climate change. Yet they will equally have to face the impacts of climate change for which they feel some recompense should be made by the main perpetrators. The moral case for this is a strong one, but richer countries are slow in acknowledging their role let alone doing anything seriously about it.

Government attitudes to climate change differ depending on which political party is in power. Behind these differences lie two different ways of viewing the world. Traditionally parties on the political left, such as Labour in the UK, believe that the state (i.e. the government) has an important role to play in providing the services necessary to meet people's needs. Parties on the right, such as the Conservatives in the UK, believe that the privatisation of services creates the greater good. In this view, it is not the role of government to provide services, such as education, water or transport, but private companies. Competition between companies, thus the term 'free-market', is seen as the way to obtain the best services available. In terms of climate change, right-orientated parties are likely to offer less direction and support, allowing the free-market to decide which initiatives are most needed. Government guidelines on climate change will accordingly often be weaker. Left-orientated parties are likely to offer more direction and support together with appropriate legislation.

It is not just politicians and governments that are responsible for decision making in the face of climate change. Whatever life we may lead it is being gradually affected by, and will be increasingly affected by, changing climate. It would seem prudent therefore to know more about the action that can be taken to mitigate, that is lessen, climate change and the action we need to take to adapt to its impacts. There are numerous international organisations concerned about every aspect of this, as well as specialist, professional, citizen, environmental, educational and community groups each with their own brief. It is this collective decision making from the bottom up and national/international decision making from top down, that collectively is beginning to make a difference. Examples of what one can do and what one can achieve together are given throughout the book, particularly in Parts 3 and 4. Whilst the issues may be daunting these are exciting and challenging times in which to live. There are many changes we can make individually and in our families. This impact can grow exponentially when individuals and communities come together to work for change in their own country and across the world.[5]

At one level, we cannot know the impact of our individual actions except that they can influence others and that influence in turn can spread wider and wider in ways that we cannot imagine. Wherever one travels one will find similar others engaged in the struggle to create a better world and many of them are now focused on what can be done in relation to climate change in their own area. Linking up with like-minded others, whether near or far, reminds us we are not alone in these endeavours, even if it may sometimes feel as if we are.[6]

## Uncertainties

There is, of course, a lot that remains to be clarified about the consequences of climate change. For example, we cannot be sure how high carbon dioxide levels may rise, how much hotter it will become and at what rate this might occur, nor for certain can we be clear about the medium and longer-term consequences of this. We do not know how quickly sea-levels will rise and the impacts this may have on coastal cities and areas. It is not clear yet what the different impacts of climate change will be around the world. We don't know yet whether all sectors of society will come together to mitigate, i.e. limit, some of the impacts of climate change. One of the key matters that the IPCC reports on is different possible scenarios for the future - what low, medium and high climate change impacts could look like. In essence they can be summarised as follows.

## Three climate change scenarios

### HIGH

- *Business-as-usual:* life goes on unchanged
- *Consequence:* runaway climate change
- *Impact:* extreme danger to society

### MEDIUM

- *Making some changes:* mostly token in nature
- *Consequence:* possibly some limitation in climate change
- *Impact:* enormously difficult times ahead

### LOW

- *Low-carbon transition:* the end of fossil fuel use
- *Consequence:* creative adaptation to climate change
- *Impact:* the only safe and efficient way forward

Another form of uncertainty comes from beginning to learn more about climate change itself. For example, all sorts of questions arise in relation to one's responsibilities at home, at school and in the community. What this book does is provide a clearer picture of what one needs to know and what one can do. In other words, it aims to support the reader through some of the next steps that need to be made, steps which involve changing our perceptions of energy, clarifying the sort of future we're interested in, understanding how to work with difficult feelings about this, learning how to adapt to climate change and how to help limit it. It also considers what a more sustainable low-carbon future could look like. In other words, it highlights insights, plans and actions that can be shared with others in the transition we are now entering towards a low-carbon society.

This is because changing climate cannot help but give rise to a wider uncertainty. We are not used to things happening on a global scale and certainly not in such a way that it will affect the lives of everyone. Neither is it an issue that just one group of specialists can resolve. It affects all specialists and all people everywhere. We need joined-up thinking where different specialists and groups communicate and work with each other. Certainly, climate change is not an issue for climate scientists alone to sort out, indeed it is beyond their power to do that. It is an issue to be lived with, one which we may be able to limit to a certain extent and which we will certainly have to adapt to. It will bring out our differences as well as our similarities, differences between countries, cultures, age groups, genders and politics, and similarities in that people will face a range of dilemmas, from moving home to changing their means of livelihood. But human beings are also expert communicators, explorers, adaptors, inventors, poets, artists, inspirers and mentors with a wealth of insight and expertise, both known and not yet known, such that all sorts of things can yet be achieved. As environmental educator David Orr comments, 'The plain fact is that the planet does not need more successful people. But it does definitely need more peacemakers, healers, restorers, storytellers, and lovers of every kind. It needs people who live well in their places. It needs people of moral courage willing to join the fight to make the world habitable and humane.' [7]

It is also important to recall that in any discussion or debate about climate change a range of perspectives is likely to be present. This is not to do with climate change as such but is a broader fact of human life. Our views will vary depending on age, gender, class, politics, culture, ethnicity, religion and nationality. This is one of the truths of human existence. How we resolve and work together on the issues that face us is a different matter. As noted above, in relation to international conferences, one of the key debates is about how to apportion responsibility for climate change and the consequent costs of this. Thus poorer countries have pointed out that they played a much smaller part in the creation of global warming than did the richer industrialised nations. Whilst to the latter it may be seen as fair that everyone contributes equally to the costs of climate adaptation and mitigation it does not feel like that to many African and Asian countries. For them this is not a question of being difficult but one of climate justice and responsibility.

This first chapter has set out, in as straightforward a way as possible, some of the basic things one needs to know and understand about how and why the climate is changing. One can go on to explore this in as much detail as one wishes and an indication of important sources of information are found in the notes and references at the end of the book. This chapter has been about opening one's eyes, although your eyes may well have been open already. One needs to know first, what the news actually is even if it's uncomfortable, so one can then choose how best to respond in order to keep one's family and community as safe and secure as is possible. You now have some of the basic information that you need and further chapters will elaborate in positive ways on some of the options and possibilities before you. I hope by the end of this chapter you've found something that catches your attention and which you would like to follow up. There is much in the following pages that can lift the spirits by showing how people are rising to the climate challenge and working together in inspiring and exciting ways to create a more positive future.

## 2. What's energy got to do with it?

*Energy is what keeps us - and our way of life - going. It is something we tend to take for granted. As long as there is electricity in the wall sockets and petrol in the pumps, most of us are not worried about how our electricity is generated.*

- David Buchan, writer on energy issues[1]

As if climate change wasn't enough why is it necessary to understand something about energy too? Energy bills always seem to be going up and we're always being told we should change providers to get the best deal. Energy, its uses and impacts come into it because it is the other side of the climate change coin. They go hand in hand and one cannot be understood without the other - it's that simple. Each sheds light on the other. Neither issue would exist without the other.

Energy is what makes the world go round whether it's the sun ripening crops or the fruits of our own personal labours. Throughout recorded history we have searched to find and experiment with various, different forms of energy. For most of this time the options were limited - energy could be provided by humans, animals, levers, pulleys and simple tools. The richer you were the easier it was to obtain vast amounts of energy to build, for example, the great pyramids or daunting castles and rich cities. Slave labour or indentured labour was often freely available. Horses, carts and carriages, oars and sails, watermills and muscle were the order of the day and great feats of the imagination were brought into existence by these alone.

What transformed these age-old forms of energy and the societies that went with them were the Scientific and Industrial Revolutions of the seventeenth to nineteenth centuries and, in particular, experiments with steam. Steam engines to pump water out of mines, steam to drive locomotives, steam to power ships, steam to power industry. What exciting times of change these must have been and beyond all previous dreams. Energy was suddenly abundant and the fuel that created the pressure provided by steam was abundant coal. Coal and steam power transformed Victorian England and much of the world, followed by oil and gas. All three are fossil fuels and have a significant carbon impact.

## High-carbon energy

### Coal

Coal has been described as fossilised sunshine. In a geological period called the Carboniferous age, giant fern forests proliferated, lived and died. During their lifetime, they soaked up vast quantities of carbon dioxide as trees do today. When they finally fell, it was often into swampy ground where they decayed and were gradually buried. Over the millennia that followed these once huge fern trees were crushed and overlain by other sediments from ancient seas. They simply became part of the geological record. Where these rocks later outcropped at the surface it was found that, broken up, they could burn and provide heat. Crude mines developed in such places and in some places coal became prized as a domestic fuel. With the rise of the steam engine coal was suddenly in huge demand, it became the fuel of the industrial age. It held its supremacy from the end of the nineteenth century, when it supplanted wood as a fuel, to the middle of the twentieth century, when it was in turn supplanted by oil.

Without coal, we would not have had the wide-ranging industries, the mines, railway networks, global routes (merchant, passenger and naval fleets), products and processes which bound the country and the empire closer together in the nineteenth century and enabled Britain to lead the world. Coal was like gold, bringing wealth and prosperity wherever it was found and wherever it went. It did not, of course, bring wealth and prosperity for those who hewed it out of the earth although it did for the masters who oversaw its production. A significant part of its downside lay in the lung diseases it produced and the grime and pollution it created wherever it went. At the time this was often seen as a regrettable and minor side-effect of this profitable source of energy. Although the health problems associated with coal working became well known what was not realised until the later part of the twentieth century was the effect of its burning which releases carbon emissions into the atmosphere.

Whilst coal was largely replaced by oil as the fuel of choice in the mid-twentieth century, it has of late seen an unanticipated resurgence. One of the main reasons for this is because it is cheaper to produce as a fuel than oil or gas and there is increasing demand for coal from newly industrialised countries. However, of the three main fossil fuels, it is both the least likely to run out and the most damaging to the atmosphere. In the US, the tops of mountains are blasted away to create vast opencast mines and globally demand is as high as it used to be in the 1960s. Using coal to meet our energy demands plays a major part in on-going global warming.

*Oil*

Like coal, oil has been known about for centuries and used as a lubricant, a sealant and even for flame throwing in ancient warfare. Both oil and gas are found in rocks from the Jurassic period when microscopic plants and animals sank to the bottom of the then seas forming a layer of organic material in the mud. As this eventually turned to rock so oil and gas deposits were formed. It was originally taken from pools where oil had seeped to the surface. Early drilling for oil began in America in the latter half of the nineteenth century when it was widely used as a lubricant and lamp fuel. By the first decade of the twentieth century half of world's oil production was being used as fuel for the increasingly popular and attractive internal combustion engine.

During the first half of the twentieth century electrification changed the world. Electricity is a carrier of energy, not a source of energy, but its multiple uses greatly boosted the need for more and more coal and oil-fired power stations. The big oil companies, such as Exxon, Texaco, BP and Shell became global giants in the twentieth century. From the middle of the last century the revolution in car ownership went from a relatively small number of individual people to often multiple ownership by families. The car became an object of worship and veneration, as any car advertisement still demonstrates. At the same time transport systems the world over sprang up, from bus and tram to rail and air. Oil fuelled not only a transport revolution but also a materials revolution with its many by-products, from plastics and fertilisers to loft insulation, DVDs and many other staples of everyday life.

Cheap and plentiful oil became the hidden life-blood of industrial society but, as with coal, burning it to satisfy our material needs also put carbon dioxide into the atmosphere. What has become increasingly clear is that there seem to be no new untapped large oil fields. Oil exploration peaked in the 1960s and production may have already peaked or be about to peak in the near future. We are moving therefore from what one might call an age of 'easy' oil into one of more 'difficult' oil, difficult in that oil is becoming harder and more costly to extract from sensitive environments such as the Arctic or deeper waters such as the Gulf of Mexico where the BP disaster occurred in 2010. Extraction in Canada is also increasingly damaging vulnerable environments, such as the Athabasca tar sands.

More recently a breakthrough has been declared through the use of hydraulic fracturing (fracking for short) where companies drill vertically down into shale rocks and then out horizontally over large distances to obtain oil or gas. High pressure fracking fluid is pumped down to crack the shale and sand particles are used to keep the fractures open. Oil or gas then flows into the pipe and up the well. Significant public opposition has arisen from this with concern about groundwater contamination and the right to drill beneath people's property and land. Whilst the US has achieved oil self-sufficiency in this way it seems that although well production is high at the beginning it often tends to fall off rapidly, making the life of the well a short one. Using oil to meet our energy demands plays a major part in on-going global warming.

## Gas

Much that has been written about oil also applies to gas in that it is a lighter version of oil and often found in association with it. Although also known in ancient times it is the latecomer of the three main fossil fuels, only really becoming part of the global energy mix in the 1960s. In contrast to oil, new gas finds still exceed production. Its prime use is in relation to power generation where it is a highly efficient fuel. It is, however, more costly and expensive to transport than coal or oil. Gas-fired power stations are quicker and cheaper to construct than coal-fired ones. One of the stated reasons for fracking for gas in the UK is that it produces lower carbon emissions than coal or oil. Whilst on the one hand this may make some carbon sense it is nevertheless an energy source which still contributes to global warming.

## Nuclear

Whilst the uranium used in nuclear power stations creates no carbon emissions these plants nevertheless present future society with several problems. They are the cost and length of time they take to build; the radioactive nature of their fuel source uranium; the hazards of storing highly dangerous radio-active waste safely for centuries into the future; the safety of such waste in the face of sea-level rise and extreme weather. Despite major accidents in the past, such as the meltdown at Chernobyl in Russia and the flooding at Fukushima in Japan, some see nuclear power as the fuel of the future, particularly the nuclear industry. Since nuclear power doesn't contribute to global warming some politicians see this as an answer to the energy gap that will occur with the retreat from other fossil fuels. Whilst this may be the case others argue that the resultant dangerous nuclear waste which lasts for thousands of years is not something future generations would wish to inherit.

These then are the main fossil fuels which have come to power the modern world. All are the subject of considerable debate in the context of climate change. Coal, oil and gas may feel like old and trusted friends, but now we can see them for what they are, both more and less than they seem - much more dangerous and less user friendly than they appeared. Globally, coal is responsible for 43 percent of carbon emissions, 36 percent is produced by oil and 20 percent from natural gas. Two-thirds of the world's carbon emissions actually come from only ninety big companies, such as Chevron, Exxon and BP.[2]

## Divestment

In order to keep below the key figure of a 2C rise in average global temperature it is vital we begin to reduce our use of fossil fuels as soon as is possible. Given the now recognised hazards relating to their use it is not surprising that various initiatives have emerged aimed at limiting their use and demanding investors withdraw their support from fossil fuel companies, particularly coal and oil. This movement received crucial support when researchers at University College London pinpointed both the type and location of fossil fuels that would need to be left unburned in the ground if the world is to avoid dangerous climate change.[3] The consequence of this for major fossil fuel companies is their oil and coal reserves would become worthless. The research shows that coal, the most polluting of the fossil fuels, would be hardest hit with 82 per cent of today's reserves needing to be left in the ground. This would mean major producers such as Australia, the US and Russia would be unable to use 90 percent of their reserves. A third of existing oil reserves would need to be unburned, which is the equivalent of Saudi Arabia's own reserve. While the prospects are better for gas 50 percent of reserves would still have to stay in the ground, much of this being in the Middle East and Russia.

82 percent of existing coal reserves must stay in the ground

This analysis calls into question the vast amount of government and private investment that goes into exploration for new fossil fuel reserves. This investment is opposed by groups such as the Fossil Free campaign and is why financial experts, such as the Bank of England and the global investment bank Goldman Sachs, are concerned that fossil fuel initiatives could become worthless. Other supporters of divestment include UN head Ban Ki-moon and former UK government chief scientific advisers, whilst Jim Yong Kim, World Bank Chief, has called for an end to fossil fuel subsidies. Many university campuses have been looking at their own institution's investment portfolios and called for divestment from fossil fuel companies. Glasgow University was the first in Europe to do this and many others are following suit. The Rockefeller Foundation in the States, itself founded on oil wealth, has also begun its own gradual programme of divestment. Other organisations which have begun this process include the World

Council of Churches, the British Medical Association, city councils such as York, Hackney, Reading and Oxford and some 800 other global investors.[4]

The big fossil fuel companies, which have often supported climate change denial and opposed green energy initiatives, are increasingly seen as a rogue industry lacking in moral legitimacy. For this reason the reduction in financing fossil fuels has begun. What is also beginning to happen is that investors are switching to much cleaner and less dangerous sources of energy which are at hand, sources which point the way to the only safe and clean alternative we have, a low-carbon economy.

## Low-carbon energy

But, if fossil fuels have become so integral to modern life, how can we possibly do without them? Fortunately, there is a suite of alternative energy sources at hand which are already beginning to spread globally, sources which were first pioneered on a small scale back in the 1970s. Low-carbon energy is clean, abundant and renewable - principally solar, wind, water and biomass. Detailed studies of these sources can be found in Godfrey Boyle's authoritative book *Renewable Energy: Power for a sustainable future*.[5] These are the sources which are now being developed, and have been for some time, to replace the dangerous use of fossil fuels. Countries vary in their degree of take-up and in the mix of renewable sources they have chosen to develop to meet their needs. Political parties also often differ in their degree of allegiance to such a goal (see chapter 1). Central to the shift to a low-carbon economy is the need to cut carbon emissions in order to avoid runaway climate change. The UK Committee on Climate Change in their fourth report recommended a 50 percent cut on 1990 levels by 2025 and a 60 percent cut by 2030.[6]

### Solar

If all the solar energy arriving at the earth's surface was caught and saved, the electricity it could generate would meet our needs many times over. Historically, solar energy was used to heat rooms directly and to create fire, but it was not until the late nineteenth century that the notion of cells which could store solar energy was explored. The first really effective silicon photovoltaic (PV) cells were developed in America in the early 1950s and became an accepted source of power for satellites. Early rooftop arrays for electric lighting and telecommunications appeared in the 1970s and the first solar power station and solar car in the early '80s. By 2000 large-scale production of solar panels had become increasingly common.

Solar energy is available not only via photovoltaic cells which create electricity but also for heating water and to drive turbines. Solar thermal energy is used to heat tubes containing a liquid which transfers the heat to a hot water tank. This has been particularly taken up by countries with sunny climates which lack other energy alternatives. Concentrated solar power (CSP) uses mirrors to focus the sun's energy onto a liquid which boils water, with the resultant steam driving an electricity-generating turbine. The largest solar power plant is located in the Mojave Desert in California.

Over the last twenty years or so rooftop solar photovoltaic panels have begun to proliferate, whether on homes, village halls, offices or schools. Whilst governments have varied in their financial support for solar energy, start-up grants and payments of a feed-in tariff began to encourage interest. Whilst some politicians have proved cautious in their endorsement, more progressive incentives for home owners, schools and businesses should steepen the take-up curve. Solar farms, with a large number of panels at ground level, have begun to spring up. France's largest 90 megawatt solar farm, launched in 2011, has 113,000 panels covering an area of 500 acres in the Alpes-de-Haute-Provence region. The largest solar farm in the UK, so far, is at the decommissioned Jane Wheal tin mine near Truro, a 1.4 megawatt farm set in an area due to be developed as a green business park. Globally 2013 saw record-breaking growth for solar electric generation as both PV and CSP markets continued to grow.

## Wind

Wind power has a long and ancient history in the powering of mills, often for grinding corn but also for draining low-lying land as in the Netherlands. Given the UK's windy weather on and offshore wind-farms with their many turbines have a major role to play in the transition to a low-carbon economy. Those who find such developments visually intrusive seem not to understand the wider cultural shift that needs to take place in relation to carbon choices and energy security.

The modern wind turbine industry, both on and off-shore, was pioneered in Denmark. Wind has proved to be the most successful renewable electricity source to date. The technology is well understood and the costs of electricity production are coming down. The taller the turbine the greater the wind speed it is likely to capture, which is one of the reasons for the erection of off-shore wind farms. The first commercial wind farm in the UK was built in 1991 at Delabole in Cornwall. The best-known UK offshore example is probably the London Array in the outer Thames estuary with its 175 turbines. These produce 630 megawatts of electricity, which is enough power for nearly half a million homes a year. Wind is now the UK's largest source of renewable energy generation and provides nearly 8 percent of the country's electricity generation. The World Watch Institute notes that, 'With decreasing costs of operating and maintaining onshore wind farms, onshore wind-generated power is already cost-competitive with conventional power energy sources in many markets.' [7]

It should be noted that onshore wind power has its detractors who, for a variety of reasons, misunderstand the urgent need to cut carbon emissions. The drawbacks they cite are damage to natural habitats, spoiling the countryside in rural areas, lack of consultation and what were seen as inappropriate government subsidies to the industry. Whilst these are concerns which need to be taken into consideration, they are overridden I believe by the urgency of climate change. Nevertheless, a number of Conservative critics want a moratorium on further development of wind power, a move which should be resisted. In 2015 the Conservative government in the UK prematurely announced cuts to the incentives given to these vital industries, both solar and wind.

## Water

Water mills were recorded in the Doomsday Book in the eleventh century and played an important part in our economic history. Today water power more generally has a vital role to play in the form of hydropower, wave power and tidal power. Hydro has long been used in mountainous areas where water is fed by gravity from high catchment areas via pipes to turbines at the foot of the valley. Hydropower only works in sufficiently rugged areas where there is high rainfall and a significant drop to the generating turbines below. The UK is the undisputed leader in the development of marine energy and there are many opportunities for wave and tidal power to be developed given the length of the coastline. Up until recently water power in this form saw much less investment than other renewable forms of energy. It has been argued this was partly due to an early wave project being evaluated unfavourably by a panel which included experts from the nuclear industry, whose financial interests gave them quite a different view on UK energy priorities for the future.[8]

Experiments in producing wave and tidal power have lagged somewhat behind developments in wind and solar energy; in part this is due to the much more rugged construction that is needed for underwater features. Important centres of development are the European Marine Energy Centre in Orkney and Wavehub in Cornwall. Since many countries are landlocked interest in this renewable source of energy tends to hit the headlines less frequently. The best known tidal barrage, built in the 1960s, is that on the river Rance in Brittany. Here a road-bearing dam crosses the river where the rise and fall of the tide is used to generate electricity. Wave power is more difficult to capture for the simple reason that waves are more chaotic and multi-directional. One of the first examples was created in the 1970s by the UK pioneer of wave power Stephen Salter.

Wave power creates energy that can be used by a turbine in different ways. The tidal stream turbine at Strangford Lough in Northern Ireland has two underwater rotor blades which turn so it works rather like an underwater windmill. Ramsey Sound off the Pembrokeshire coast is the site for testing a different and newer tidal stream unit. The Pelamis Sea Snake, on the other hand, is made up of sections which flex and bend as waves pass and it is this motion which is used to generate electricity. A planning application for a tidal lagoon at Swansea Bay is currently under consideration. In Cumbria, an area of mountains and high rainfall, new micro hydropower schemes are providing electricity to local villages. Different forms of water power are thus gradually appearing offshore in coastal areas and on rivers and streams. The Department of Energy and Climate Change has calculated that around 20 percent of the UK's electricity could come from wave and tidal sources.

## Biomass

This refers to the burning of wood, straw and organic material to create energy; it includes scrap timber, forest debris, some crops and manures. This is a renewable form of energy in that such residues are widely available. Drax, the big coal-fired power station in the north of England, has converted part of its plant to run on biomass. There is a problem, however, if such timber is as a result of deforestation in different parts of the world.

Globally renewable energy sources saw their fastest growth in 2013 and provide 22 percent of the world's electricity. The International Energy Agency expects the power generated from renewable sources worldwide to exceed that from gas and be twice that from nuclear by 2016.[9] Energy from renewable sources is expected to increase by 40 percent over the next five years. It is now the fastest growing energy sector and by 2018 likely to make up a quarter of the global energy mix. In Denmark renewables already provide 26 percent of the county's energy.

Surveys for the Department of Energy and Climate Change (DECC) show that over three-quarters of UK adults support use of renewable energy sources to generate the country's electricity.[10] Support for use of individual sources is as follows:

- solar (82%)
- wave and tidal (73%)
- off-shore wind (72%)
- onshore wind (67%)
- biomass (60%)
- nuclear energy (36%)

## Making the transition

If politicians and economists get their act together and provide thoughtful leadership, guidance and support to communities, a managed transition to a low-carbon economy can be made. A number of different scenarios could occur, of course, from the carefully planned to the chaotic.[11] One of the key principles in a more sustainable low-carbon society would be a fundamentally different attitude to energy. Energy will need to be used more thoughtfully and sparingly. There will be less energy available to waste and squander than has been the case under a fossil-fuel regime. Commentators thus often talk about the need for a planned 'powering down'. Energy will need to be more thoughtfully used and more wisely directed. John Urry, in *Societies Beyond Oil*, points out that it took society some fifty years to bring about significant reductions in cigarette smoking despite the known dangers, adding 'We can presume that a similar time would be needed to power down high-carbon societies given the enduring power of carbon capital'.[12] Powering-down, he points out, relates not just to the economy but to society as a whole. Whilst the thought of this might seem alarming the crucial upside is that the major reduction in carbon emissions will help mitigate the impacts of global warming. It is a big shift which is why the new low-carbon story needs to be bold, positive and possible.

The World Bank reports that by most measures of human development Cuba is now more or less the leading country within the developing world. Cuba has systematically disregarded neoliberal recommendations as to how to bring about economic and social recovery. Cuban life expectancy is almost identical to that of the USA but overall Cuba only uses about one-tenth of the USA's energy per person.[13]

## Reflection

So, the short answer to the question posed by this chapter - 'What has energy got to do with it?' - is actually 'Everything.' To understand anything about climate change we also need to understand about the sources of energy available to us and the impact they may have, positive or negative, on both people and the environment. There have been many periods in history when new ideas and insights began to challenge the accepted ways of doing things. Major historical revolutions, such as that from water power to steam power, did not happen overnight. The dilemma we face in the early twenty-first century is that we don't have an infinite amount of time available in which to make such a shift. Procrastination, whether in the form of delay, postponement or even denial, will only leave our children and grandchildren with difficult tasks that we should be undertaking now.

The UK led the way in the first Industrial Revolution which took us from water power to coal and steam thus transforming our world. The UK could help champion a second such revolution in this century, moving us away from high-carbon fossil fuels towards a low-carbon economy based on clean and renewable sources of energy. Still to be commercially developed in this area are methods of storing such energy which, unlike that from fossil fuels, is variable, i.e. intermittent, rather than constant in its availability. A low-carbon economy will certainly be based on a mix of renewable energy sources as well as a smart power grid that is less centralised than at present given the widely dispersed sources of generation.

It is difficult to comprehend the shift in available energy that came with fossil fuels, a shift we take entirely for granted. In trying to clarify what this energy jump from human labour to mechanical means looked like Richard Heinberg suggests we imagine this as having our own personal 'energy slaves'.

> Suppose human beings were powering a generator connected to one 150-watt light bulb. It would take five people's continuous work to keep the light burning. A 100-horsepower automobile cruising down the highway does the work of 2,000 people. If we were to add together the power of all the fuel-fed machines that we rely on to light and heat our homes, transport us, and otherwise keep us in the style to which we have become accustomed, and then compare that total with the amount of power that can be generated by the human body, we would find that each American had the equivalent of 150 'energy slaves' working for us 24 hours each day.[14]

I suspect a British citizen would have fewer 'energy slaves' than the average American but this still succinctly sums up our historical energy position. In today's materialist and consumerist driven society we have the equivalent of many more such slaves than our parents or grandparents had. Is it possible that the abundance of cheap fossil fuels, especially oil, over the last hundred years has encouraged us to live beyond our means? By that I mean have we taken the notion of progress essentially to be about acquiring material wealth rather than, for example, human well-being? Whilst standards of living may be rising slowly across the world there is still an increasing gulf between rich and poor, not least in the UK.

How might we fare in a low-carbon society based on renewable energy sources? The immediate advantages would be improvements in human and environmental health as the 'side effects' of coal and oil production decrease. A low-carbon economy would be cleaner, healthier and safer for us and our children. In the face of possible disruption to present often distant energy sources, gas from Russia for example, renewable sources can provide much greater energy security for the country as well as requiring new engineering skills and the creation of many jobs.

# 3. What's the choice of futures?

*Our interest in the future is part of human beings' habit of putting themselves into a narrative - if possible, one that encloses an individual life in a larger story. A book which is looking forward ought to see how far into the future we can make the story go.*

- Jon Turney, science writer[1]

Why think about the future? Well, the first reason is that we're likely to be spending quite a lot of time in it. We have a personal reason as it were. Whilst some are happy to just wait and see what happens in their personal future we do still spend quite a lot of time thinking about it and planning for it. Have I bought that birthday present yet? Is it time I booked the holiday? Will life feel different when I'm 40? Will I ever have grandchildren? These are all questions or at least passing thoughts about our personal future. There may also be actual or proposed developments going on in your local community. Do you feel these will enhance community well-being or hinder it? At a national level, we are offered various versions of the country's future by different political parties. Which does one trust to create a fairer and safer future?

## Thinking about the future

So we are all engaged in thinking about the future in different ways. An important reason for this is so that one can be prepared for different eventualities that may come about. This may relate to personal, local, national or even global futures. In times of rapid and troubling change it is easy to lose one's bearings and for life to feel more uncertain. It is useful therefore to set time aside sometimes to think through particular issues or important choices that need to be made. Doing this will certainly have an effect on one's future and so it should be time well spent. Whilst decisions are made in the present the consequences that follow are in the future, whether that is in minutes, days or decades. So thinking about the future is important. We often do this incidentally but it can also be helpful to sit down and do it consciously and deliberately. A key advantage of this is that one will be better prepared for what may be to come and it will be good for oneself, one's family and community.

We generally talk about the future (singular) rather than futures (plural), some quirk in the English language perhaps. It's very useful to talk about futures in the plural because, at any one point in time, a number of different possible futures could actually come about. It is a reminder that the future is not fixed but flexible and open to change. Our actions, individually and collectively, have an impact on the future. The present that we live in is the result of innumerable conscious and unconscious decisions made by people over recent decades and centuries. It is also true that we do not have equal power in helping shape the future. Whilst global companies, financiers, economists and politicians have a lot of power and influence over the future compared with individuals, so do groups of ordinary citizens when they choose to work collectively together in movements for positive change.

Many organisations and professionals are concerned about different aspects of the future, from climate scientists and economists to Non-Governmental Organisations (NGOs) and activist groups. Challenges that will affect the near future, for example, range from genetic medicine and artificial intelligence to climate change, resource depletion and food shortages. Global trends, all of which have local impacts, are monitored regularly by the Worldwatch Institute. Here are some examples:

- Growth of global solar and wind energy continues to outpace other technologies

- Agriculture and livestock remain major sources of greenhouse gas emissions
- Automobile production sets new record, but alternative vehicles grow slowly
- Development aid falls short, while other financial flows show rising volatility
- Peacekeeping budgets equal less than two days of military spending [2]

If each of these trends continues to deepen I wonder which you would consider to be part of helping create a better future? Which trends do you feel need enhancing and which reversing? How might they each impact on your own life and community?

One of the most useful distinctions futurists make is that between probable and preferable futures. Since the future is not clearly known it is still a flexible place. However, some futures are more likely to come about than others given current trends and events, and are thus labelled probable futures. They are futures we *expect* to come about. This can hold true at different levels from the personal to the global. As mentioned above it is past and current trends and events that that help shape the future. Futurists and others thus analyse and project local, national and global trends to ascertain their possible and probable impact on the near, middle and long-term futures.

Preferable futures are a quite different category of future. These are the futures we would most *hope* to see come about based on our deepest values and beliefs. When humanity has made great progress it is often because of the tireless work of many individuals and groups working for positive change, even if it doesn't occur in their lifetime. The abolition of slavery, the eradication of illiteracy, votes for all, the creation of the NHS, greater protection of the natural world, all of these came about because people had a dream, a vision of a better future for society. It is important to recall that we benefit from the visions our parents and former generations struggled to bring about for the future well-being of society. Every generation surely has a responsibility to do the same.

So the difference between probable and preferable futures is really important. Where it looks as if we're going may not be the same as where we'd actually like to get to. In some cases your probable future may also be a preferable one because of your careful planning in order to bring this about. On a global scale climate change is more than just a probable future because its impacts are being felt now. On a national scale one might note that social commentators have observed the UK becoming more individualistic, materialistic, less caring and tolerant over the last thirty years. This trend has been driven by the views of some leading economists and politicians who believe everyone is responsible for their own fate, that competition solves everything and that support from the state is an obstacle to progress.[3] Unless seriously challenged such a trend is likely to lead to greater inequality and intolerance in the UK.

Visions of a better world can sometimes be unrealistic, they may never get off the ground or they may fail ignominiously. But they may also come about in another form or they may be created by the next generation. Truly great ideas may need long periods of gestation and may be picked up by future generations to realise. What is crucial in the context of climate change is having a positive vision to plan from and work towards - and we know that in this case it needs to be a low-carbon future. If we can't imagine what this might look like and what a society needs to do to create it, it will be impossible to get there. This is why being able to clarify what a safe, clean and healthy future looks like is of vital importance to all of us.

Being able to think critically and creatively about probable and preferable futures, whether personal, local or global is a valuable life-skill in difficult and fast changing times. From the middle of the twentieth century onwards the probable future, we were told by politicians, scientists and economists, was also the preferable future. Economic austerity, growing inequality and global warming may make us want to review that argument. Whilst it is true that a person's probable future can also be their preferable one, increasingly today what seems probable feels far from preferable. It is vital, therefore, that we distinguish between the two.

Past, present and future are also connected through the different generations in a family as shown below. Here in the present we may know people who are in their nineties or even older. In that sense we have connections that go back a hundred years. Similarly, babies born today may also live to a ripe old age, so we also have connections that may go forward in time for a hundred years. It is thus argued that whilst the present moment may last for a fleeting second it can also be seen as a 200-year moment because of these generational connections. What have older generations passed on to us? What in turn do we wish to pass on to the future?

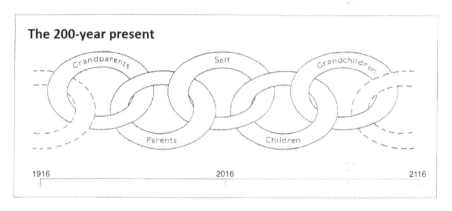

**The 200-year present**

Grandparents — Self — Grandchildren

Parents — Children

1916      2016      2116

## Sustainable v. unsustainable

There are many frameworks that can be used to help understand the issues we're facing today. Of particular value in the context of climate change is the concept of sustainability, the meaning of which, however, has been somewhat muddied since its emergence in the 1980s. As Engelman observes:

> We live today in an age of *sustainababble*, a cacophonous profusion of uses of the word *sustainable* to mean anything from environmentally better to cool. The original adjective - meaning capable of being maintained in existence without interruption or diminution - goes back to the ancient Romans. Its use in the environmental field exploded with the 1987 release of *Our Common*

*Future*, the report of the World Commission on Environment and Development.[4]

This original meaning cited above is the one this book adheres to. The muddying of the waters came from two main directions. Firstly, increasingly popular usage of the term watered down its sense to mean something vaguely 'green' or generally good for the environment. Secondly, many big corporations and politicians took over the term to signify their alleged commitment to the principle - a process known as greenwashing. In this context anything could be described as 'sustainable', from airlines and oilfields to office practice or making slightly more effort than usual over something. No wonder some people are confused. So, yes, there has been debate about the use and value of the terms sustainable and unsustainable. Some argue they have been used so loosely that they have become meaningless. For example, when a fossil fuel company talks about sustainable mining they mean mining that will give the biggest profits for as long as possible. All mines have a finite life and many other resources are also finite and unreplenishable. So it's important to listen carefully when this term is used to judge whether it is being used loosely or has been deliberately co-opted. A colleague recently told me I shouldn't use the term sustainability because its meaning had become so clouded. It reminded me of a time in the 1980s when the word peace became a political football. If one spoke of 'peace' during the superpower nuclear arms race between the USA and the Soviet Union it was taken by some to indicate one was a communist at heart. However, as a History HMI (Her Majesty's School Inspectorate) said to me, 'The word 'peace' needs reclaiming and filling with meaning.' The same, I believe, is true of the term 'sustainable.'

At the simplest level a process or practice is considered sustainable if it can bring well-being to people and the environment over a long period of time. Alternatively a process is unsustainable if it is causing harm or damage to people and the environment. Take forestry for example. If one cuts down more trees than one later replants this is unsustainable forestry, one fells and then moves on elsewhere. When forest cover is removed in this way it can lead to greater run-off and flooding and the loss of trees that would normally soak up carbon dioxide from the atmosphere. It may be a win for the logging company but not for local communities. Replanting as many or more trees than have been felled is an example of sustainable forestry. There will be timber to cut in the next cycle, slopes are protected from heavy run-off from rain and carbon dioxide is absorbed from the air.

Fisheries are another example. In many parts of the world seas have been nearly fished to extinction by the practices of large commercial fishing fleets. Everything that can be caught, large or small, has been taken and those not considered of value thrown back. This decimates the fish population which may take years to recover or not recover at all: an unsustainable process. Sustainable fisheries look to long-term outcomes. To ensure a constant supply of fish one needs to limit both the size and the amount that is taken. If the size of mesh on the net lets young fish go free they will live to reproduce and replenish. If the amount taken is also appropriately calibrated fishing can go on almost indefinitely, it is sustainable. Both of these cases, and many others, highlight the disadvantages of short-term exploitation of a resource with little or no concern for the future.

Major disquiet about the impact of human activity on the environment hit the headlines in the 1960s and 70s. Rachel Carson's book, *Silent Spring*, which explored the widespread impact of pesticides on wildlife was decisive in generating this concern.[5] Organisations such as Friends of the Earth, Greenpeace and the Sierra Club in the US contributed to the emergence of a growing environmental movement, as did the 1972 UN Conference on the Environment. In particular the Club of Rome's report, *The Limits to Growth*, showed that if current global trends continued there could be major problems ahead for society in the twenty-first century.[6] It was the widespread blossoming of environmental concern in this period which later led to the emergence of sustainability as a key organising idea in this and other fields.

What is encouraging today is the way in which issues of sustainability are now seen as infusing all areas of life. There is a wealth of distinguished practice, past and present, to draw on which is both informative and inspiring.

A good example is Wayne Visser's, *The Top Fifty Sustainability Books*, the front of which displays each of the book covers in miniature.[7] The text highlights the most influential writing in this field over a forty-year period demonstrating the durability of the concept and its many applications. So the notion of sustainability is not a new idea but a well-honed and well-used concept. Each of the books dealt with is explored in just a few pages, including a synopsis and bullet-point list of key ideas. It's not a book that needs reading all at once, but rather one to be dipped into and relished. A companion volume sets out key sustainability initiatives and events which also occurred over that forty-year period. This is the history we can draw on in exploring and explaining issues of sustainability today.

## Environment, society and economy

Whilst early definitions of sustainability focused on environmental matters it soon became clear that the concept could and should be applied much more widely. For some time now, it has therefore been taken to embrace the three vitally interrelated areas of life below.

- *Environment:* for example air, water, land and living things
- *Society:* for example well-being, education, equality and justice
- *Economy:* for example work, business, finance and trade

The point one must start from and to which one must continually return is the planet itself on which we live. When I first argued this, quite a long time ago, one colleague called me an old hippy, implying this perspective was a bit odd. It was, however, in the 1960s, a powerful new image - the first ever photographs of the

Earth from space. Our home planet had never before been seen from off-world and it immediately filled one with the deepest awe and wonder. What is absolutely crucial to our well-being and indeed all life on the planet is the functioning of the biosphere. Given the pressures of daily life it may take some effort to grasp this bigger picture but it's essential for our survival and all that we love.

> The biosphere - the sphere of life - is the living part of the outermost shell of our rocky planet, the part of the Earth's crust, waters, and atmosphere where life dwells. It is the global ecological system integrating all living beings and their relationships. Peoples and societies depend on its functioning and life support while also shaping it globally.[8]

The problem in relation to the biosphere is that so many people have no idea of its role in allowing life to exist on the planet and the services it provides which we take so for granted. This is why the bottom line for any human activity is whether, knowingly or unknowingly, it damages the biosphere and degrades the free services that this life support system offers. A parallel would be living in a room with very heavy smokers over a long period of time whilst imagining this couldn't possibly have any impact on one's health or the air quality in the room. Whilst staying with this analogy it is worth remembering that the big tobacco companies, against all the evidence, steadfastly denied for many decades that their product was injurious to health.

Taking the well-being of humans and the natural world as vital to life would seem a good ethical position to start from. What I would wish for myself I should also wish for others. When we talk of the natural world we're actually talking about the biosphere, that narrow layer of atmosphere, land, water, flora and fauna which surrounds the world and is our life-support system. If that were not present there would be no life on the planet. The Earth's biosphere is the equivalent to the skin of an apple in its depth. If we imperil this, our life-support system, we imperil ourselves, our children and all of life. In the twenty-first century there is no excuse for ignorance of this. So, in thinking about preferred futures, it is vital to bear in mind what a more sustainable society could actually look like and how this is already being created in different communities.

The biosphere is immediately visible to us in the natural world. It is not surprising that native peoples lived in awe of this, given that one's livelihood depended on it and its moods. It is not surprising that such people respected, worshipped and wished to propitiate the forces of nature that were beyond their control. This changed in the eighteenth and nineteenth centuries when European inventiveness suggested that man should be the measure of all things and used that power to control nature and the natural world. At that time one could not have imagined the twentieth century consequences of this. But we now know differently. We ignore or try to dominate different aspects of the biosphere - plants, creatures, earth, air and water - at our peril. Our relationship to nature is central to the predicaments we face today. In the nineteenth century the Romantic poets, such as Wordsworth and Coleridge, understood this and stood against the spreading industrialisation and urbanisation of their time. Many others have done so since then. Whilst Richard Mabey in the 80s felt the great English language tradition of nature writing had died of neglect, some twenty years later he could celebrate its renaissance.[9]

I used to ask my students, many of whom would become geography teachers, when they had first become aware of the natural world. When they paused to think about this they were back in their childhood, jumping in puddles, excited by icicles, smelling flowers, running in woods, paddling on beaches, climbing trees, listening to the bees. When I asked them what feelings they associated with these experiences they came up with excitement, joy, fun, inquisitiveness, enjoyment of the senses, astonishment, longing and passion. When I then asked them where those feelings were as adults they looked a bit sheepish and embarrassed, finally mumbling that these were childhood feelings not adult ones. I suggested this needed to change as one of the aims of education is to instil and develop a sense of wonder in the child. How could they do this without being able to find their own?

Education, both formal and informal, has a vital role to play in nurturing this sense of wonder, passion and excitement and keeping it alive. To feel this deeply is to intuitively understand what sustainability is about and to act responsibility in relation to the natural world. Being outdoors in interesting and exciting natural environments is something young people deeply enjoy. It nurtures body, mind and soul. The other side of the coin is that with this sense of pleasure comes a responsibility to protect and nurture the natural world, without which there would be no life on this planet at all.

Exploring the Lake District fells

Societies are complex human systems which can vary enormously over time and space. A sustainable society is one characterised by higher levels of equality, cohesion, cooperation, justice and well-being, to the benefit of all. Conversely, an unsustainable society would demonstrate higher levels of inequality, fragmentation, conflict, injustice and ill-being, to the detriment of many. This is one of the reasons why a number of indexes of social well-being have been developed in order to assess the societal quality of life. The Happy Planet Index, for example, has three components: life expectancy, experienced well-being and ecological footprint, and is applicable at national levels.[10] This results in quite a different picture of societies and ranking of countries to the increasingly old-fashioned GNP (gross national product). Wilkinson and Pickett's work on material success and social failing in modern societies also demonstrates that more unequal societies are bad for the well-off as well as the poor.[11] A more sustainable society or community is a safer, fairer and healthier place in which to live.

It is with economics that one runs into the greatest difficulties - the field of knowledge that deals with the production, distribution and consumption of things. Human impact on the environment can occur in many different forms but the form of economics we choose to follow has the biggest impact of all. This is because the raw materials to create all the stuff we have and use come initially from the natural environment. Its production and distribution impact on the natural environment as do the sort of commodities we choose to produce.[12] The disposal of such stuff also impacts on the natural environment. Increasingly many economists like to think their subject is a science, but in actuality it is no such thing. Its form is deeply influenced by the values its proponents hold, thus free-market economics, welfare state economics and green economics are each driven by differing value beliefs. They may all be about how production, distribution and consumption work best, but beyond that they are entirely different creatures. A more sustainable form of economics makes a major distinction between *more* (excessive consumption) and *enough* (maximising well-being) and why the latter is more beneficial to people than the former.

Free-market economics has become the dominant form of economics over the last forty years. It is based on the belief that the 'market' should not be subject to any national or international control but free to evolve in its own way. Thus inventors, entrepreneurs, financiers, banks, businesses and industry all play a vital part in the market. It is said that what the market reflects is what people rationally choose to buy. A product is 'good' if lots of people choose to buy it and 'bad' if lots of people don't. Advertising, of course, plays a major part in the decisions that people come to, itself a subtle psychological game to make people always want more. There are no ethics in such a system, one which encourages big businesses globally to go where wages are lowest, environmental legislation non-existent and profits high for their shareholders. More than three million Bangladeshi workers in garment factories produce goods for export, mainly to Europe and North America, in unsafe working conditions at rates far below a living wage. As if this was not enough a large proportion of the population, living in the vast river delta area of Bangladesh, live only inches above a rising sea level.

One therefore needs to know something about what more sustainable ways of living look like in practice, one which does not cause damage to others, wherever they may live in the world, or to the natural environment. At the same time one needs to oppose unsustainable activities, those that cause harm to others or the natural environment. Recognising the activities that have a dangerous effect on people and the environment and working to minimise these is part of sustainable living. The way we understand and live our lives in the light of sustainability issues will vary from person to person. Some are inspired to help create a more sustainable lifestyle (treading lightly on the earth) and work thoughtfully and imaginatively to create this in their own lives and communities. Others are shocked by the unsustainable practices they see around them (treading heavily on the earth) and spend more time working to transform such practices. Many do both as the two courses of action are equally important. Whilst significant damage has and is being done there are many researchers, activists, NGOs and others working to protect different aspects of the environment at local, national and international levels.

In this context, as well as climate change, it is important to highlight loss of biodiversity and the limits to growth. It is known that in the geological past, before humans arrived, there were five major periods of mass species extinction. Whilst these were caused by volcanoes, asteroids and sudden natural climate change we are now heading towards a sixth mass extinction this time caused by human activities. Between 1970 and 2010 the population of vertebrates (any creature with a backbone) has halved over this forty year period, land creatures by 39 per cent, freshwater species by 76 per cent and marine species by 39 per cent. This is as a result of agriculture, industry, deforestation, pollution and urban growth. Such loss of biodiversity is the equivalent to seriously damaging vital bridge supports and imagining this will not affect its structural safety. If we can't actually tell how far the damage has gone or what the overall effect will be it doesn't bode well in terms of future safety.

At heart we are damaging the planetary life-support system because we ask too much of it and dump too much waste into it. Either would be serious errors of judgement in any other life-support system as earlier examples of forestry and fishing showed. Asking too much relates to our use of the Earth's re-sources to satisfy our needs, whether that is clean water, more roads, more energy, more buildings, nicer clothes or greater speed. In fact the quantity we desire may be more about our wants than our needs and there's a vital distinction between the two. Fulfilling my basic needs for food, health, company and being loved is different from wanting a new car, the right clothes, a better house and more stuff. As Gandhi noted, 'The world has enough for everyone's need, but not for everyone's greed'. In today's world needs and wants are commonly confused and the mantra now seems to be that people want more of nearly every-thing. Indeed many believe that constant growth is the answer, whether in economies, businesses, possessions or popularity. Much of this has been driven by the deliberate rise in consumer-ism fostered over the last thirty years. Whilst Roman citizens were given 'bread and circuses' to keep them in their place, today we are bought off with slick advertising and celebrity game shows.

## A sustainable society

I have used the well-established concepts of sustainability and unsustainability as tools to explore the options we face today and the choices we need to make, whether personally, in the community or at a planetary level. The twentieth century saw great technical and scientific progress at all levels of society, yet great inequality still exists and damage to the natural environment continues to increase. Rather than enhancing human and environmental well-being, which is what we had hoped we were doing, this has been at the expense of the planetary support-system. Things must now change and we can all be part of those changes. Even if climate change was not occurring, given the long-standing unsustainable hazards that the old ways have created, we still need to move towards a more sustainable society without delay. And, as this chapter has stressed, this must embrace the interlocking sectors of environment, society and economy. The good news is that we have some fifty years of analysis, research and good practice to draw on. In the face of climate change, to move towards a safe and clean low-carbon economy, will require all the insights and expertise gained from this fruitful history. In this context Haydn Washington observes:

> We have seen that our economy is broken, our society is broken, and that the ecosystems that support us are breaking. Also ... we delude ourselves that 'everything's fine'. Yet the interest in 'sustainability' within society today shows that many of us (at least in our inner hearts) realise that everything is not truly fine. So sustainability is the task of *healing these broken things*. This is what a meaningful sustainability should be. It has to be about creating a culture that lives in harmony with Nature (and each other) into the future.[13]

This is why we are faced with a choice of futures and why we have to think more widely and more deeply about the sort of future we would wish for ourselves, our families and communities. In order to limit climate change and adapt to the changes it brings we need not only a low-carbon economy based on renewable sources of energy but also one which acknowledges the limits to growth in a finite world. Living sustainably needs to become our norm, one which respects and protects the planet we live on and those we share it with. What an exciting challenge to work on with others.

# Part Two

## Telling new stories

.

# 4. The old story: high-carbon

*It's all a question of story. We are in trouble just now because we are in-between stories. The Old Story - the account of how the world came to be and how we fit into it - sustained us for a long time. It shaped our emotional attitudes, provided us with a life purpose, energised action, consecrated suffering, integrated knowledge, and guided education ... We could answer the questions of our children. But now it is no longer functioning properly, and we have not yet learned the New Story.*

- Thomas Berry, cultural historian[1]

So what have stories got to do with climate change? Well, quite a lot really as we will see. One way or the other we all like stories because life is full of them - stories we enjoyed as children, family stories, adventure stories, romantic stories. Stories can embody great truths but can also contain hidden lies, they can be fictional or taken from real life. Telling a story can mean exactly that, but it can also mean something make-believe or untrue. Stories, both fictional and from real life, can also help us find our way in turbulent times. They provide something to hold on to so that we don't give up hope or get lost. They can give direction. The notion of story is a rich and compelling one which can help clarify the choices we face over climate change, energy futures and the well-being of our communities.

## Why stories matter

Stories involve times and places, characters and plots which unfold with twists, turns and consequences. Expectations are heightened and diminished, characters succeed and fail, a turning point or climax occurs, hopefully leading to a resolution.

There are happy endings, tragic endings and surprise endings. Stories can be found in books, newspapers, online, and in our own heads and hearts. We tell stories to ourselves, we rehearse things, conceal things and imagine things. In the wider sense there are social stories, cultural stories, political stories and economic stories which also hold our lives together. They influence much that we do and take for granted because they are so deeply embedded in our subconscious we often don't know they're there.

When I learnt about the Greek myths at school I felt sorry for the ancient Greeks because they believed their stories to be true. When we talk about something being a myth we often mean it's untrue. Much later I learnt myths can contain fundamental insights and profound truths about the nature of the human condition. Carl Jung was one of the first to identify the archetypal or universal images that many myths contain, images and symbols which can evoke deep responses in a reader. Such stories often involve quests, initiations and descents into the underworld. They have familiar characters such as the Hero who saves the day, the Scapegoat who takes the blame, the Outcast ejected from the group, the Mentor who offers good counsel. There are also archetypal situations: a great task which needs performing, a quest to find something precious, loss of innocence through new knowledge, initiation into a different world. These characters and situations raise questions about the meaning of life, they capture profound truths about the nature of being, society and the cosmos.

So stories come in many shapes and forms and they matter because, even if not realised consciously, they help us explore our thoughts and emotions and instruct us about issues we may have to face and resolve. Understanding something about the power and value of stories can help us make more sense of the times we live in and the problems we face. Here I'm taking two sorts of story to shed light on the position we're in and the challenges we face - the notion of ideology and of cultural narrative. These are not as dry as they may sound but useful tools for digging deeper into things. The term 'ideology' has been used with varying meanings over the years, but the sense in which it is used here is as follows.

> Ideology is defined as a broad interlocked set of ideas and beliefs about the world held by a group of people that they demonstrate in both behaviour and conversation to various audiences. These systems of belief are usually seen as 'the way things really are' by the groups holding them, and they become the taken-for-granted way of making sense of the world.[2]

The notion that collectively shared ways of viewing the world work at both conscious and unconscious levels is a valuable one and helps explain the differences and clashes that occur in many debates and disputes. One can talk, for example, about differing political ideologies (beliefs about how society works best), economic ideologies (beliefs about how prosperity is best achieved) and educational ideologies (beliefs about the purposes of education). This is an important reminder that these and many other areas of human endeavour are contested, i.e. people hold quite different beliefs about what is 'right' and 'best' and thus fight (sometimes literally) to make their belief system, which they take as normal, the dominant one. When I used to introduce this notion to my students they often wrongly said 'Yes, that's right everyone is different', taking this to be about individual differences rather than a set of views collectively shared with others. Of course, some ideologies may become dominant in a society, although not necessarily held by every-one, and so people begin to experience their particular set of beliefs as just 'normal' and 'common sense'.

Cultural narratives are an example of ideological differences on a large scale. They are the stories that a culture tells itself about its beginnings, history, achievements, purposes and goals. They are 'self-evident' truths taught in childhood or picked up by osmosis in one's society. Whilst these may be modified over time they often become the unassailable threads that help bind a culture together, the truths by which one lives. Some elements of the

British cultural narrative would be the importance of Magna Carta in declaring the king was not above the law, the fact that the Industrial Revolution began in England, the vast benevolent Empire we once ruled over, how the country stood alone in the Battle of Britain and won, the importance of democracy and fairness in all things. Such elements are also contested but contribute generally to what one might call a grand taken-for-granted historical narrative. In exploring where we are today we need to take a look at where we've come from. In looking at some of the key cultural themes that have emerged in the west over the last three-hundred years or so we can get a better purchase on why the present is as it is.

## A cultural story

Historians generally note a distinct difference between life during the medieval period and that which came after. Some see this as a series of revolutions, others as more gradual transitions. During the sixteenth and seventeenth centuries, what is often called the Scientific Revolution began to alter how people saw and experienced the world. A great burst of intellectual activity during this period laid the foundations of modern science and also how we thought of ourselves. Developments in astronomy, anatomy, medicine, botany and engineering, laid much of the foundations for modern science and technology. The influential French philosopher René Descartes argued that mind and matter were two quite separate things and that identity should be equated with the rational mind. Isaac Newton, who set out the foundations of physics, saw the universe as a mechanical system governed by mathematical laws. Even God sometimes became thought of as an engineer or a clock maker. Mechanistic philosophies, those which saw the world as being rather like a complicated machine, began to stress the importance of order and control in order to make things work effectively. The older medieval view of the world and nature as an organic whole faded away to be replaced by a new unifying model for science and society - the machine.

During the eighteenth century the Enlightenment played a crucial role in furthering this growing scientific view, a view which is still held by many today. Enlightenment thinkers, following on from the exciting developments of the previous two centuries, particularly valued what they called 'critical rationalism'. By this they meant the application of reason (rather than emotion or religious thinking) to resolve social, political and economic issues. This, they agreed, would lead to the further improvement of humanity, a revolutionary and radical idea at that time. Underlying this view of life and society were other supporting beliefs: that reason and rationality were the key to all knowledge, that science was the key to all things, that reason and science were universally applicable in all situations and that through the application of reason and science progress would inevitably occur. What an exciting time to have lived in, what new insights awaited discovery! Science came to be seen as the pinnacle of enlightened reason because it seemed to be the key to all endeavours and it promised control over harmful aspects of nature making change something to be welcomed rather than feared. The purpose of life now became framed by a belief in the inevitability of progress.

The Industrial Revolution that was to follow occurred over a hundred-year period from the mid-eighteenth to the mid-nineteenth centuries. It was fuelled by the Scientific Revolution and the powerful Enlightenment thinking that had preceded it. The significance of the Industrial Revolution is enormous since this was when the foundations of the modern world were laid down, a new world driven by a coal-fuelled economy and continuous technological innovation. In the latter half of the eighteenth century a crucial network of canals had been built which hugely improved the movement of goods and the acceleration of trade. The crucial breakthrough came with the development by Thomas Newcomen of a steam engine which could pump out the water that frequently threatened to engulf mines. The next step was the development of a more efficient steam pump through the work of Scottish inventor and engineer

James Watt. Richard Trevithick was the first to use steam to power a locomotive. As steam engines improved so did the range of their uses in factories, forges and mills, where innovations in spinning and weaving encouraged the growth of the textile industry. It was the cotton industry in particular which marked the rise of British industry in the nineteenth century. Coke, a by-product of coal, was used in the manufacture of iron and steel, materials essential to the spread of industry, manufacturing and the development of an industrial economy.

With George Stephenson's development of the steam locomotive, first used by collieries, both people and goods could be transported more quickly than by coach or canal which in turn encouraged the spread of settlement as it became easier to move from place to place. The Stockton and Darlington Railway opened in 1825 and a dense rail network soon grew up across the country. Whilst it was steam that provided the power for the Industrial Revolution it was dependent on readily available coal as fuel. Then in its turn coal mining became a major industry. Up until this point, and throughout this period, water still provided extensive power for mills and the canals which were the A-roads of their day, carrying goods across the country more safely and quickly than the road system of that time. These developments led to a growth in manufacturing which, with improving transport systems, spread across the country and began to revolutionise trade internally and internationally. Brunel's steamship, the Great Britain, was launched in 1838.

By the end of the nineteenth century coal was king, fuelling the greatest railway network in the world, power stations, merchant shipping and a navy that controlled the seas and connected the far-flung British Empire. Coal gas was used for heating and lighting and other by-products gave rise to the chemical industry. Steam remained the dominant power source throughout the century, and coal was the fossil fuel that transformed the world. In 1800 annual world output of coal was 15 million tons a year; by 1900 it was over 1700 million tons, mostly from Europe and North America. Without the use of coal the Industrial Revolution and the modern world would probably never have occurred. Its use and expansion led to previously unknown levels of prosperity as people demanded more goods and a more comfortable life. Roger Osborne observes, 'The Industrial Revolution was, in essence, the transition from an organic economy to an economy based on energy derived from fossil fuels, as well as the beginning of a sustained period of innovation that has lasted to the present'.[3]

Coal and steam powered this Victorian express locomotive

But, towards the end of the century, the successor to the steam engine had begun to appear, the internal combustion engine, fuelled by petrol and diesel. At the time the impact that oil would have on the world could not possibly have been imagined. The decline of coal began at the beginning of the twentieth century and, whilst still important, mines in the UK continued to be closed and the industry was finally broken up by privatisation in the 1980s. Today the UK's coal is imported from abroad and currently provides about 40 percent of our energy needs. As the internal combustion engine began to come into its own oil became the dominant fuel of the twentieth century. Production from oil wells in America had long been used as kerosene for lighting and the first oil refineries and oil companies appeared in the 1860s and 70s. As oil discoveries grew in the new century so did the demand for fuel for cars and then aeroplanes, further confirmed by the needs of both World War 1 and World War 2. By this stage the giant international oil companies had come into being as well as the discovery of large oil fields in the Middle East. In the United States and other industrialised countries standards of living rose continuously, based on the availability of cheap oil. As coal had dramatically shaped the economic, political and social landscape of the nineteenth century so oil was to do the same in the twentieth. Life became inconceivable without it. Not that one woke up in the morning rejoicing at its availability, but that it was always there in the background, providing fuel, warmth, light, fertilisers, pesticides, plastics and innumerable other everyday items from bank cards to CDs.

As a result of mass production and advertising in the economic boom of the 1920s a culture of consumerism emerged. Items such as cookers, washing machines, vacuum cleaners and cars made life easier and allowed greater leisure. After World War 2, as consumerism began to become the norm, it became seen as a social and economic ideology in its own right. From the 1970s onwards, as this way of life became even more deeply entrenched, the term was often used to mean excessive levels of consumption well in excess of one's basic needs. Come the early twentieth century Neal Lawson argues we moved from consumerism to turbo-consumerism.

> Consumption once meant tuberculosis. Now it means 'to use up'. A society defined by consumption 'uses up' on a systemic and industrial scale. Indeed, while it isn't all we do, the culture, institutions, laws and values of society are now organised primarily around consuming.[4]

Annie Leonard explores in depth the ways in which this obsession with stuff also creates intricate and complex webs of damage that affect the biosphere, our life-support system, our communities and our health.[5]

This is the story that most of us grew up with, a story of improvement and progress as a result of human ingenuity and the triumph of science. It was ultimately the Industrial Revolution that led to the historical breakthrough in which humans gained control of their world. That notion of control, however, also involved both European colonisation of other countries and stripping them of their assets for our gain, and similarly viewing the natural world as an apparently inexhaustible source of resources and somewhere to dump our waste. Nor, of course, did everyone benefit equally from the fruits of the Industrial Revolution whether initially within the UK or more globally. So what therefore have been some of the consequences of this period of history and the cultural narrative that has been constructed from it?

## Some awkward consequences

We have, amongst other things, become addicted to fossil fuels, first to coal and then to oil but, like many addictions, this was partly because for a long time we didn't understand their use involved dangers we couldn't know of. As there was once a time when it was fashionable to smoke cigarettes - they were even considered to be good for one's health - so we did not understand that fossil fuels, coal, oil and gas, held a dangerous secret. We knew in the case of coal that it brought problems such as polluted air, wasted landscapes and damaged lungs, and with oil the death of oceans, coastlines and wildlife. What we did not understand was that the gases released in their use, their burning, were ones which could seriously upset the balance of the atmosphere. Why might this have been so?

This is where we need to return to the notion of cultural narratives, the tales we collectively tell ourselves about the purpose of life and its meanings, something humans have struggled with from the beginning of time. Leaders, politicians, economists and others have all contributed to this narrative in different ways. The dilemma, however, is that since we've absorbed a particular historical narrative about the meaning of life from the day we were born, we generally don't see it as a story but rather as normality based on unquestionable truth. This is why in these times when we face the challenge of climate change it's important to ask, 'Where have we come from? What are the cultural narratives we've grown up with that seem so normal they've seldom been subjected to questioning? '

This is why cultural historians and other commentators try to assess how the past has helped create the present we find ourselves living in. This is why taking the long view is really important. By looking at some of the key ideas that underpinned the Scientific Revolution, the Enlightenment and the Industrial Revolution, we can begin to see how these narratives have affected our views of life and society today. Some of the beliefs we've internalised from our forebears and which many take as self-evident are the following.

- That science can help us solve nearly all known human problems if we only put enough thought and money into it.
- That such thinking needs to be rationally and scientifically based in order to produce beneficial results.
- That if we hold to this we can continually improve the human condition. This is called progress and this is what life is really all about.

That we have achieved amazing things and great benefits in human well-being is without doubt. From Victorian times onwards a good standard of living has been largely marked by consumption of material things such as property, clothes, vehicles and other goods. At different times different items are considered more or less important and, in particular, fashionable. Clearly a person's income has a direct effect on these matters and the greater inequality there is in a society the greater the dissatisfaction there will be. This also raises the question of what might be meant by enough?

So, if with hindsight and in the face of climate change, we take the long view, how might we see some of the benefits and disbenefits of the cultural narrative many have grown up with? This is not to judge our forebears but to take a view that would not have been possible for them in their own time. Looking back at the Scientific Revolution we might note that the mechanistic worldview, the breaking down of things in order to better understand the parts, brought much greater and deeper understanding. It was a vital step in scientific thinking but we're still often better at taking things apart to learn about them than understanding how things work and interact as a whole. Ecologists remind us that everything is connected to everything else and that if we forget this we can cause untold damage to both society and the environment. As well as understanding the different pieces of a jigsaw we need to understand how things fit together to create the whole picture. The Enlightenment thinkers took some of these scientific ideas and their principles further, especially that the use of reason alone could resolve all dilemmas. At the time this way of thinking emerged it was indeed a great step forward. It was a more scientific way of doing things than before, a major leap in western ways of thinking.

Today we might point out that the heart and emotions have an equally crucial part to play in understanding ourselves, life, work and society, the vital other side of the coin, as indeed the Romantics emphasised at the time. Also that science is only one way of examining the world and what happens in it. The Industrial Revolution, building on these ideas, made it possible to change extensively both the material and natural world, to build and create, to invent and improve, better manufacturing, better transport, greater well-being, improved communications, greater wealth and order in society. Today we are rightly impressed by all that happened then, material progress was one of the gifts of our ancestors which laid the foundations on which the modern world is built. It is also important to note that Victorian society was a time of great wealth and great poverty. That the benefits brought by all these changes were unequally distributed, that we used our military might to create an empire and used its people and resources largely for our own benefit.

For most of human history man-made climate change was not a possibility. But looking back at the nineteenth and twentieth century we can now see that the coal and oil on which this progress was built had an unseen poison in its tail, that the use of fossil fuels brought many benefits but at a high cost to present and future generations. Our ancestors could not have chosen differently because they did not have, could not have had, the scientific insight available to us now. Only now can we begin to put the pieces together to see the broader picture. Only now can we see the wider costs and consequences of what were seen as great ideas, developments and improvements at the time, improvements which have brought great material and social benefits, although not for all, and without which modern society as we know it would not exist. The task of present generations, whether one would wish it or not, is to deal with the terrible sting in the tail of fossil fuels on which this 'progress' has been built. The only question we can really ask is, 'Are we up to it?' Previous generations had to face the rigours and horrors of World War 1 and World War 2, a trauma I cannot begin to imagine. And yet it has been said the challenges we face in combating climate change are as great as the collective effort needed to defeat the Third Reich in the 1940s.

So this is the point our cultural narrative or story has brought us to. Not story in the sense of being fictional, not story in the sense of being untrue, but story in the sense of being a set of powerful and exciting ideas about who we are, what we're part of and what we might do next. Such ideas are like an underground stream that seeps into the public consciousness to become the largely unquestioned backdrop to our lives like the air we breathe. Of course there are always those who challenge such ideas but they are often marginalised or seen as dissidents. The elements of our cultural story as outlined here help us make sense of the world but at heart this is a high-carbon story, high-carbon because our dependence on fossil fuels led to the carbon emissions that create global warming. As a schoolboy I enjoyed watching films about coal mining and oil exploration in geography. These discoveries all felt very exciting, we were fuelling a new world and, I indirectly learnt, men in white coats, i.e. scientists, were going to solve all known human problems! That may sound foolish now but it was part of the world I grew up in and absorbed then without a second thought. At the same time many people today still believe technology can solve any problem. Technology, however, is no better than its creators (mostly male) and can be used for good or evil - and sometimes what looks to be good also turns out to be malign.

## Rethinking the story

If we stand back from this cultural story, perhaps now better seen as the Fossil Fuel Age or high-carbon story, we can see it is underpinned by two powerful interrelated themes - the notions of conquest and progress. These have been key threads in our narrative from the seventeenth century onwards, elements which are also common to much of the western world. The excitement felt by the movers and shakers at the time of the Scientific Revolution, Enlightenment and the Industrial Revolution was enormous, for those periods promised and led to great changes in society for an increasing number of people - greater comfort, greater choice, greater wealth and greater control of nature. The crucial tools that emerged from this ferment were the focus on rationalism, the new sciences and a wide range of new and innovative tools and technologies. Together they helped bring into focus the notion of progress. Where once our fates were seen as in the hands of God it increasingly became clear that these matters were now in our own hands. In the nineteenth century wherever one chose to look it appeared that life could be made better. The dream of perfectibility seemed increasingly possible and even more so in much of the twentieth century, despite two world wars.

But in what ways is progress brought about? On the one hand it is through the invention of labour saving devices, greater medical insight and skills, improved education, wiser laws and a more active democracy. On the other hand what has often been considered as progress has been achieved by subjugating the natural world, plundering its resources as if they were limitless and treating the biosphere as if we had no responsibility for it whatsoever. Similarly, people were subjugated in the name of progress and colonial empires set up in order to benefit the colonisers and bring progress to the locals. Developments in military technology may have defended freedoms but they also contributed hugely to the carnage of World War 1 and use of nuclear weapons in World War 2. Such progress appears to have a high price tag for some and is far from equal in its impacts.

Progress, however, provides an emotionally appealing narrative which goes so deep that John Greer likens it to a surrogate religion. For the true believer, he argues, this takes three intertwined forms: moral progress, scientific and technological progress and economic progress. For many it is axiomatic that these three go together but, because of this, it has to warrant closer investigation.

> It's important...to pay attention to the ambiguities wrapped up in the modern conception of progress. When people think or talk about progress, by that name or any of its common euphemisms, there are at least three different things they can mean by it. All three share the common presupposition that history has an inherent and invincible tendency to move in a particular direction, that movement in that direction is a good thing and that human beings can and should contribute to that forward movement towards the good.[6]

Moral, technological and economic progress, take many forms and, like all human endeavours, never come value-free. Moral progress would originally have been seen as Christian and today, more widely, probably seen as western. Scientific and technological progress presumes ethical ends, even if not always stated, but can range from cancer cures and prosthetic limbs to gas chambers and tools for torture. Economic progress today is believed by many to be measured by the success of free-market capitalism which, Will Hutton argues, has brought at least as much pain as pleasure to its recipients and unequally spread.[7]

So our cultural narrative, as well as the innumerable benefits it has brought, also has its dark side which we often manage to ignore. But if not progress, with its inevitable forward trajectory, then what? It is worth noting that no society or culture in history has continued for ever, despite our belief that we are different. Whether the Aztec empire, the might of imperial Rome or the colonies of the British Empire, they eventually fade away. The fact that we think we really are different today is not supported by the historical facts. We urgently need to begin questioning our cultural narrative, the three-century story that has brought us to this place, because if we don't we may not survive. We have become unwittingly addicted to fossil fuels and by ignoring the limits to growth, thinking this too could go on indefinitely, we are causing dangerous damage to our species and habitat.

This chapter began with a reflection on various sorts of stories. In many there is a sudden denouement where everything is turned on its head. The old high-carbon story, what one might call the Fossil Fuel Age, seemed to be a good guide to the future but we can now see is that in powerful ways it was a flawed and false narrative. In stories based on myth the Hero is the one who saves the day. But heroes can also be flawed, having great strengths but also a vital weakness. The high-carbon story, in many ways, embodies the myth of the Hero, but this hero also plays the role of conqueror. Indeed we often talk of the Conquering Hero and that is the myth we have lived by, whether the literal conquest of others or the domination of nature, which is then supposed to stay conquered.

I am reminded of the figure of Faust in the classic German legend who, in his unquenchable quest for knowledge, power and control, sold his soul to the devil. In doing so, however, he suffered eternal damnation. No wonder such an agreement is often described as a Faustian bargain. Our long-term use of fossil fuels would seem to have become a serious addiction because of the immediate benefits that it gives society. Satisfying addictions is all about short-term goals and the immediate now. The long-term impacts seem irrelevant and unimportant. In the face of global warming this Faustian addiction urgently needs to be challenged, as the divestment movement and others are already doing (see chapter 2). It is time for a serious rethink and a major change of direction onto a new and safer course. It would seem time for a new story and a new cultural narrative to live by. Fortunately this story has already been around for some time.

# 5. The new story: low-carbon

*If you do not change direction,*
*you may end up where you're heading.*

- Lao Tzu, Chinese philosopher[1]

The previous chapter stressed the importance of cultural narratives in helping individuals and societies make sense of their world. In particular it looked at some of the stories which have helped underpin our views of progress in the western world. Here, in the early twenty-first century, we find ourselves in a delicate and critical position because the old high-carbon story we and our forebears have lived by has now been found to have caused global heating and thus climate change. Therefore, we urgently need to identify new stories that will help us move forward in a more positive and creative direction. And, since the old story was a big and heroic one, we need something challenging and exciting to replace it. This is, of course, something that humans are good at doing. In prehistoric times our distant hunter-gatherer ancestors survived by hunting animals for food and gathering wild plants to eat. For thousands of years this was their main way of living, people invented some basic tools, painted pictures in caves and worked closely together to survive as a community. This was their story, we travel to find food, we keep on the move, we have developed the skills we need in order to do this well.

## Developing a new story

But one day 10,000 years or so ago in the Middle East someone dared to say, 'I don't want to go hunting or gathering today, I want to see if I can use these seeds to grow something of our own. And I wouldn't mind keeping a few animals too'. This was not part of the cultural narrative, the all encompassing sense-making story of the time, but it gradually began to shake up the old ways and point towards a new way of being - staying in the same place and growing your own food. The First Agricultural Revolution was beginning. It would have seemed heresy at the time, an unimaginable way of living, with the excitement of hunting and all its skills threatened. For centuries both hunter gathering and farming would have existed side by side to different degrees in different places and contexts. But slowly and probably often with difficulty more and more people settled to being farmers and skilled ones at that, learning how to store food and even accrue a surplus to trade. One of the biggest shifts in history slowly but gradually began to take place.

We are now beginning to wake up to the fact that we are in need of a new and safer empowering cultural story. The dangers we face are not on some distant horizon but beginning to occur around us now. Not necessarily all in the same place at the same time, but it's not what we're used to, not what we really want and it would be nice if things just went back to 'normal'. But now we face a new normal, so we need story tellers to come up with a new map of where we are, where we need to get to and what we need to take with us. It will particularly help if our new cultural narrative contains a clear goal to aim for, a guiding star to draw us onwards, a story that gives us direction and hope. But cultural stories tend to change gradually and those who suggest a new and different story are often seen as heretics, threatening what appears to be the safety of tried and tested customs. This time we don't have decades, let alone centuries, in which to perfect new ideas. Most people don't realise they're living out a cultural story, let alone that it urgently needs to change. We thought we were in the middle of a play about 'progress' but suddenly we've lost the script and urgently need a new one, a song-line to show us the new route ahead. We need in these times wise and experienced story tellers able to introduce their communities to a new low-carbon story. There is no middle way here because we know that continued use of fossil fuels, the continued existence of a high-carbon emission lifestyle, threatens all that we hold dear.

Now, whilst there are many actual story tellers out there, some of whom are sharing elements of that new story, there are also many writers, commentators, business people, activists and visionaries, doing similar work. The seeds of the new story are all around us and have been for the last fifty years. But of course, apart from those who sensed our direction wasn't really the best one, those tellers were only appreciated by a few and considered deranged, mad or downright dangerous by those who saw themselves as guardians of the high-carbon status quo. Most of us at some time probably wonder what life is really all about. I certainly did in my teens and twenties. In the 70s it felt as if there was more to life than my parents made out. I was on the look-out for other explanations, new possibilities, something that made a bigger sense of things, which is when I watched the documentary referred to in the Introduction. This period was also one of wider creative and critical dissent with many challenges being laid down then about current society. The cultural narrative was beginning to slip, not in relation to climate change, knowledge of which was to emerge later, but in relation to how modern society viewed and acted on a range of major national and global issues.

The 1960s was a period of social and political turmoil, much of it a reaction by younger people against what was seen as the conformity and limitations of the 1950s. This was a decade of major popular social movements - Martin Luther King and the black civil rights movement (the right to have a vote); the anti-Vietnam war movement in which the US National Guard shot protesting students on campus; the Prague Spring in which Czech citizens rebelled against Soviet communism; student uprisings and discontent across Europe and America in 1968; protest against the nuclear arms race between the USA and Russia. The world was in the process of being turned upside down by a new and younger post-war generation. On the environmental front the early 1970s saw the setting up of campaigning organisations such as Friends of the Earth and Greenpeace and the first international conference on the environment in Stockholm. At this time there was also widespread discussion about the never-ending impact of global growth. The first ever global computer simulation, *The Limits to Growth*, explored how pollution, industrial output, non-renewable resources, food supply and population might interact over the next hundred years. However the parameters were changed in different scenarios the eventual future outcome looked bleak. The study was violently attacked by free-market critics in much the same way as climate scientists have been. However, later updates using more complex models still showed there could be a pretty tricky future ahead.[2]

Theodore Roszac, in *The Making of a Counter Culture*, captured much of the spirit of those times.[3] Young people in particular were deeply concerned about the society they found themselves living in, calling into question what they saw as the myths of material progress, economic growth and high-consumption lifestyles. Those involved in what was called the counter culture, Roszac argued, actually dared envision a better future - it was time for a new story and new beginnings. The wish for a more just and equitable society in the 70s and 80s saw the emergence of many major social movements, including the anti-nuclear movement (both energy and war), the women's movement, the peace movement, the environmental movement, anti-racism and gay rights. Thousands of people at different times and in different countries took to the streets to challenge different aspects of the status quo. Gradually, in people's daily living, the workplace and the law, changes began to be made in relation to issues such as race, gender and the environment. Roszac went on to note in *Person/Planet* that:

> Sometimes societies fall apart in ways that release life-affirming energies. And what may look like anarchy from the viewpoint of the established cultural centre may be the troubled birth of a new, more humanly becoming social order... My purpose is to suggest that the environmental anguish of the Earth has entered our lives as a radical transformation of human identity. The needs of the planet

and the needs of the person have become one, and together they have begun to act upon the central institutions of our society with a force that is profoundly subversive, but which carries within it the promise of cultural renewal.[4]

What was this if not the call for a new cultural story - one which questioned existing materialistic and consumerist norms with a much more challenging view of what it meant to be human? This need to identify the key elements of a new cultural story was taken up by Fritjof Capra in *The Turning Point*. [5] Capra took an even wider cultural view, setting out key elements of what he called the old story and the shift he saw happening in society towards a new more holistic story. Holistic means looking at the whole thing, exploring and understanding how a whole system works, rather than just knowing about the parts. A simple example would be the difference between being an expert on the individual parts of a car, yet not understanding how they interrelate to create a drivable vehicle. What Capra observed was the wider shift from what he called a mechanistic view of the world, one which took things to pieces to understand them better, as in Isaac Newton's formulation of physics or the philosopher Descartes' view that mind and body were two quite separate things, to a more systemic, i.e. holistic way, of viewing the world and its problems. Rather than separate problems - for example, poverty, violence, famine, environment - the problems were, he argued, part of one larger interconnected crisis. Understanding a globally interconnected world, he stressed, requires a holistic perspective. Physicist, David Bohm, highlighted what he saw as the problem of 'fragmentation and wholeness'.

> Fragmentation is now very widespread, not only throughout society, but also in each individual: and this is leading to a kind of general confusion of the mind, which creates an endless series of problems and interferes with our clarity of perception ... The attempt to live according to the notion that the fragments are really separate is, in essence, what has led to the growing series of extremely urgent crises confronting us ... Man begins to see and

experience himself and his world as actually constituted of separately existing fragments ... [and] thus obtains apparent proof of the correctness of his fragmentary self-world view.[6]

This helps explain why historically the natural environment has become seen as an unending source of resources and a place where all manner of waste can be dumped. But a significant number of people were increasingly becoming aware that this was unsustainable, that these acts were threatening the biosphere with its inextricably interrelated parts. Many believed at the time that this was part of a newly emerging cultural story. At the very least many of these ideas felt exciting, liberating and worth getting involved with. It was a period when all sorts of new challenges were being made in relation to how modern society worked. Looking back now I realise many of those ideas were part of a new story beginning to be born. If we had paid attention to the environmental limits then we might not be in the situation that we find ourselves in today.

## Two competing world views

Stephen Sterling has examined elements of these two world views in detail to establish how their differing emphases affect the ways in which we view the world. The terms he uses to describe these different ways of thinking are 'Modernist' (the old story) and 'Ecological' (the new story). Here are some of the key elements of these two competing ways of looking at life and the world.[7]

The old (modernist) story believes there is a solution to every problem and that we can understand something by breaking it down into its component parts. The whole of something is no more than the total of its parts and most issues can best be dealt with by sorting out the offending parts. Objectivity is necessary to understand all issues and we can understand things best through a rational response. Any other way of looking at things is irrational. In this way we can usually predict the future outcome of things. This is the way most of us have been brought up in western countries. The new (ecological) story believes some solutions just produce more problems and that we need to look at the whole, and at the larger context. Intricate systems, for example the health of a human body, show just how complex the interactions of their parts can be and that actually the whole is more than the sum of the parts. This complexity is characteristic of human and environmental systems. Most issues and events are related to other issues and events and are best understood by exploring these interrelationships. So-called opposites are often in relationship, but we tend to devalue one side against the other (ecology v. economics, people v. nature, facts v. values). What we need to do is see them as in relationship rather than in opposition. Absolute objectivity is impossible and the intellect needs to be balanced with intuition and rationality with other ways of knowing, such as the aesthetic. In human and natural systems, i.e. not mechanical ones, it is often not possible to predict outcomes. It helps therefore to be more flexible, accept uncertainty and learn from change.

Both of these ways of looking at the world can be seen as important cultural stories which currently overlap. What Sterling calls 'modernist thinking' has its origins in the old high-carbon cultural narrative whilst his 'ecological thinking' is part of the emerging new low-carbon narrative. They can be found in everyday discussion, the workplace, education, the arts and scientific research, because cultural narratives change slowly and necessarily overlap. But if a new cultural narrative was indeed birthed in the 1960s and 70s where is it now?

## Counter attack

When I read Capra's *Turning Point* in the 80s it really felt as if the old mechanistic story was beginning to decline and a new holistic story was emerging. However, such profound changes in awareness and consciousness do not occur overnight, neither do they necessarily occur peacefully. Thus some time after these concerns began to enter public consciousness they came under increasing ridicule and attack. Cultural narratives are also ideologies, powerfully held beliefs that bind our lives together, such that they appear as true and common sense. That which seems to oppose the dominant mindset can then appear as ridiculous if not downright dangerous. The newly emerging story was about to be attacked in the 1980s by powerful economists and politicians who believed capitalist free-market economics was the answer to everything. When long-standing cultural stories are threatened the old guard always rally round to enforce their version of truth, thus the powerful attacks on all who challenged the status quo.

What happened from the 80s onwards was a massive counter-attack which came from free-market economists, particularly supported by American president Ronald Reagan and UK Prime Minister Margaret Thatcher. The post-war consensus that both the state and business should have a central role to play in the welfare of society was cast aside and the free-market seen as the solution to all things. In this view of society the state should interfere as little as possible with the workings of the business world and let privatisation reign in all fields of endeavour, from education and welfare to health and citizenship. It is only through this freedom, the belief goes, that society will work most effectively. Important public endeavours once overseen by the state, such as water supply, railways and telecommunications, were sold off and broken up into competing parts. Companies were bought and sold, often to investors in other countries, in whichever way gave the greatest profits to their shareholders. The old story of growth, greed and conquest became resurgent with a vengeance.

The consequence, as commentator Tony Judt observes, is a sense that something is profoundly wrong in these times. Society has become more materialistic, selfish and narcissistic; growing inequality is the norm and what was once seen as greed is now considered praiseworthy. Worship of the private sector, economic growth and the sanctification of bankers do not actually guarantee equality or freedom.[8] The economic crash of 2008 did not happen by chance, but was the result of investment bankers at the highest level believing they could successfully manipulate global money markets. The recession affects everyone, except the super rich who are growing in number, and strangely it is the public that has to pay the price of austerity in savage cuts to public services of every kind. Notions of trust, honesty, responsibility and care for others, are seen as of little importance in this model of society, qualities which are essential to the growth and maintenance of any caring community.

## A low-carbon future

We know where to look for the key principles needed to take society forwards in a positive direction for they were highlighted by commentators such as Roszak, Bohm and Capra decades ago. Taking a systems view, an ecological view, whether of organisations or life on this planet as a whole requires that we understand how the parts are interrelated and how each influences the wellbeing of the whole. The Industrial Revolution occurred over a two-hundred year period, underpinned by the earlier Scientific Revolution and the Enlightenment. What is uniquely different in the present time is that we need to take the best of the old and the best of the new to construct an exciting and challenging narrative of where we need to get to. As previous chapters have highlighted, this is not only a low-carbon society but, more broadly, a sustainable society. Here are some of the elements in the new story of the transition to a sustainable low-carbon future which are already visible around us.

### Buildings and energy

All new-build housing and other facilities need to demonstrate high energy efficiency, whilst older properties will need to be similarly retrofitted. This move towards low-carbon buildings is not only about greater energy efficiency and therefore lower energy requirement, but also relates to the carbon footprint of its constituent parts. The increasingly well-known Passive House originating in Germany has set a voluntary standard for low-carbon housing which involves super insulation and triple glazing. This results in a huge reduction in the need for space heating and cooling whilst at the same time maintaining good indoor air quality. An interesting example of such housing in the UK is the Denby Dale Passivhaus in Yorkshire (see page 103). This is a three-bedroom detached house, built to a strict budget of £141,000, and using 90 percent less energy for space heating than the average UK house. It is twenty times more airtight than a standard build. The purpose of building this house was to provide the construction industry with an easy to build template for future low-carbon housing.

Pelamis wave energy convertor at the European Marine Energy Test Centre

The main energy sources in a low-carbon society, as summarised in chapter 3, are a mix of wind, solar, water and biomass. These will be scattered across the country depending on the availability of different sources of energy - coasts, rivers, sunshine and wind. This will require what is called a smart energy grid, one that can switch between different sources when they become available to provide a constant energy supply.[9] Various technologies are also being tested, including large scale batteries, to store the considerable but intermittent supply from wind and solar farms. Germany has launched its first commercial battery plant, the size of a school gym, which can power some 2,500 homes.

## Travel and transport

There are many reasons why people need to travel and many modes of transport but some of them, such as petrol and diesel vehicles, are high-carbon emitters because of the fuel they use and the sheer number of people that own them. In a low-carbon society fewer journeys will have to be made and more of those on efficient forms of public transport. Reducing the number of journeys made will result in reduced energy demand and therefore greater energy savings in relation to transport. Quick and efficient public transport systems come in a variety of forms from train, coach and bus to tram and light rail. When they are appropriately designed to meet public needs they can provide an efficient and effective low-carbon alternative. It goes without saying that when these and other systems use electricity as their energy source it must be from renewable sources.

Many towns have already been redesigned to make safe walking and cycling a priority in their centres. An efficient and regular bus service to meet local needs should mesh with train and coach services for longer journeys. The Netherlands has long been extolled for its stress on cycling as a norm rather than for the few. Cars will be part of a low-carbon transport system and many car makers are now producing increasingly effective electric vehicles (EVs) as well as hybrids which combine an electric battery with a standard engine. The engine recharges the battery, which operates at low speeds, and also has very low carbon emissions. Electric charging points for EVs are becoming a more common sight, as in Newcastle, and should eventually be everywhere. In a low-carbon future cars might simply become part of the scenery rather than, as it is for some, an addictive source of excitement.

## Consuming and wasting

One of the problems to face in the transition from a high to a low-carbon future is the unsustainable way in which the Earth's resources are being used. This has become expressed in terms of Earth Overshoot Day.[10] If we were using the planet's resources sustainably our annual needs and wastes would match the carrying capacity of the Earth. Once we are using more than is available we fall into what ecologists call overshoot. What is troubling about Earth Overshoot Day, the day when we've used up our annual quota of the Earth's resources, is that the rest of the year represents our carbon emissions and unsustainable depletion of minerals, forests and fisheries, which together seriously damage our life support system. Overshoot day has come earlier each year - in 2011 it was September 27, in 2012 August 22, in 2013 August 20 and in 2014 August 19. On this basis we are using up the equivalent resources of 1.5 planet Earths each year.

It is clear from this and other work on our 'ecological footprint' that we consume more resources than are sustainably available and we emit more waste than the planetary system can absorb.[11] This is one reason why household recycling in our communities is important. If something can be recycled we do not need to commit new resources to replace it. In a low-carbon future we will be aware of the whole mantra which is rethink, refuse, reduce, reuse, recycle. So there are four vital steps that come before one leaps to recycling as the best answer. Reusing things and reducing what we needed were probably last seen on any serious scale during World War 2 when things really were tight. In a low-carbon society we would actually have learnt to refuse anything we thought might contribute to overshoot and actually start from a point where we questioned everything in relation to its sustainable or unsustainable impact on both people and the environment.

## Food and farming

In a low-carbon world both food and farming will look different. Two main reasons for this relate to changing weather (more extremes) and the need to reduce food miles, the carbon emissions that arise when transporting food from producer to the market. A warming climate in the UK will make some traditional crops ungrowable but open up other new markets. Crops may need to be drought resistant and also able to stand up to heavy rain. The same will be true of livestock, raising issues of water supply and the need for dry cover. Warnings have also been issued about the need for the UK to become more self-sufficient in food and less reliant on fruit and vegetables from abroad. In the early 1990s the UK was nearly 87 percent self-sufficient in food but by 2012 the figure was 68 percent. At the National Farmers Union conference in 2015 a new report suggested that only 53 percent of the country's food needs would come from UK farms in the near future, a trend that is best reversed. Much of our fruit and vegetables that come from abroad could be grown at home.

Farming is one of the main sources of two greenhouse gases that have received little mention so far because carbon dioxide is the most common. Nitrous oxide has around a 300 times larger impact on global warming than carbon. It is released during the manufacture of fertilisers. Methane has 25 times the impact of carbon and is released from the digestive systems of cattle and sheep and from manure and slurry. In a low-carbon future farms will have decreased their carbon footprint by making fertilisers more efficient, increasing nitrogen uptake by crops and using anaerobic digesters to convert organic waste into biogas for the generation of electricity and heat.[12] An interesting development at a smaller scale of production in the UK has been the growth of Community Supported Agriculture, a social enterprise idea based on active partnerships between farmers or food growing projects and their local community. This benefits both farmers and the community in reconnecting people with the land where their food is grown. Contributors make a regular financial contribution to their scheme and take greater responsibility for how food is produced and distributed. Such schemes vary greatly in form. The Oak Tree Low Carbon Farm, for example, lies on the edge of Ipswich in Suffolk where members help grow and produce a weekly supply of fresh vegetables without use of artificial fertilisers or pesticides.

## Biodiversity

Biodiversity is the term used to describe the variety of life on Earth, ranging from insects, birds, fish and animals to plants, trees and micro-organisms in the air, water and soil. The greater the biodiversity the healthier our life-support system, the biosphere, is. Climate change causes animals and plants to migrate to habitats that are more suitable for them. This is one reason why previously unseen fish are now appearing in the waters off the UK. 'Fish and chips' is beginning to take on a new meaning. It is not only global warming which impacts on the biosphere but many other activities, such as mineral and timber extraction, overfishing and dumping of toxic wastes. There is a limit to how much the natural environment can absorb without becoming toxic and unfit for life.[13] So what we do to the environment has to be thought through much more carefully rather than being left unthought. This applies, personally, locally and globally. We may not *see* the actual damage, but it's still there. In the geological past, mass extinctions such as that of the dinosaurs, occurred when massive changes took place in the chemistry of the seas or atmosphere. In the distant past there have been five such extinctions. Scientists are now talking of a massive 'sixth extinction' of species caused this time by humans themselves.

A sustainable and low-carbon society will be constantly vigilant about the quality of land, air and water as the source of life for all its inhabitants. This ecological awareness will be demonstrated in a respect for all aspects of the biosphere from the local to the global. Many schools and educational programmes do this already, taking young people out into the natural environment to develop a sense of adventure, respect, wonder and responsibility.

This should become the norm again in a sustainable low-carbon future. Gardens, communities, fields, rivers, and all that live therein will be appropriately protected as part of the vital jigsaw of life.

The above are some of the elements increasingly beginning to appear which help make up a more sustainable low-carbon society. All of these issues, and more, have been the subject of deep concern and committed positive action for many years. Violent conflict, injustice, inequality and environmental damage are all symptomatic of unsustainable practices and processes. More peaceful, more just, more equal and ecologically aware practices and processes are characteristics of a sustainable low-carbon future. Leaving fossil fuels in the ground is only part of it. This is not necessarily an easy journey but, in the face of changing climate, these are the principles we need to begin to live by. Both home and education are vital in this process because they are where these principles need to be modelled on a daily basis. They also need to be enshrined in legislation, so that the qualities we need to survive are demonstrated from above as well as below in society. This is why one of the first Well-being Goals of the Welsh 'Well-being of Future Generations Bill' is to create 'an innovative and productive, low carbon emission economy, that makes more efficient and proportionate use of resources...' [14] The necessary changes are gradually now beginning to appear in law.

# 6. Feeling the way forward

*It is common for people to experience a range of emotions and psychological reactions when faced with information about environmental threats and predictions of an uncertain future.*

- Australian Psychological Society[1]

Previous chapters have looked at some of the basic information needed to understand issues of climate change and energy and the way in which these are embedded in two different cultural stories. This chapter returns to climate change to explore how people often feel about this difficult issue. Whilst it is frequently thought that it is knowledge that gives us the answer to things it is important to remember that feelings give us access to a different way of understanding and making decisions. For example, we don't choose a partner just on what we know about them but in particular on what we feel about them. Our choices and actions are influenced by both head and heart. Emotions can be powerful, they can lift us up, reduce us to despair or we can refuse to acknowledge their existence. This chapter explores some of the feelings that arise when people first learn about climate change, when they may acknowledge its existence, experience its impacts or go into denial about its reality.

## Why is it so difficult?

'It's scary,' she said to me, 'I don't know what I don't know, should know, and haven't got time to know'. These are the sort of feelings that come up for a lot of people when the issue of changing climate is raised. It certainly did for me and I remember thinking, 'Do I really want to know about this? Have I got room for it in my life?' The person I was talking to then asked me how I felt about this, so I took a moment to get in touch with what I myself was feeling. I realised I felt nervous, uncertain, fearful, angry, wanting to blame someone - an interesting list of feelings I wasn't sure I wanted to share. Later I realised one of the reasons I felt uncertain was because climate change makes the future feel more worrying and thus my fearfulness about what it might bring and my anger because I wanted someone to blame. At that point I could have dismissed those feelings as unhelpful and getting in the way. But then I wondered what would happen if I trusted them, was the heart telling me something important the mind could not? So what can we learn if we listen to feelings about climate change?

One of the problems we face in western society is that troubled feelings such as these are not things we normally talk about. It's not something one actually does. It might look as if I'm a wimp. Even worse, I might get upset if I let myself experience such feelings. This is often the case for many men in western culture, where the image of ourselves we've grown up with is that we have to be strong or at least should appear to be, 'I can handle this, there's no need to make a fuss, let's sort it'. Or even there isn't a problem in the first place. In all societies people are socialised in different ways, in particular when young we pick up what is considered acceptable and not acceptable behaviour from those around us.

Keri Norgaard, a researcher who wanted to find out what people thought and felt about climate change, focused on a small rural Norwegian town where she talked to people, listened to conversations, went to meetings and generally observed what the population talked about.[2] It certainly wasn't climate change. She found that if this topic was brought up it was a conversation killer. It was something outside the sphere of normal life. Climate change wasn't seen as being a local issue. What she also realised was that in a way the whole community was complicit in this and realised that people avoided thinking about climate change because it led to feelings of helplessness, guilt and deep insecurity. If you don't think about it you're not going to have difficult feelings about it. This is what psychologists call 'denial', a sub-conscious process which we use to keep painful things at bay. She observed that the emotional management techniques people used to avoid discussion about climate change were particularly pronounced amongst educators, men and public figures. Individual denial thus became social denial so that it became 'impossible' for people to engage in any discussion about climate change at all. The unspoken norms, which we have unknowingly internalised, can thus control notions of what is allowed or not allowed in different social situations.

One reason why climate change is difficult is because it raises troubled feelings that go against cultural norms. Such norms are embedded in wider belief contexts - social, cultural, political and economic. Thus embedded these protective strategies are difficult to see and identify. Not responding to climate change comes about through the social and cultural norms of everyday life. These interconnected norms are like unwritten internalised laws which control what we feel it is appropriate to pay attention to, feel and talk about. Challenging such norms often makes people feel uncomfortable. This is why bringing up climate change often stops conversation short. At the heart of the process of denial is control over the emotions. As emotions are difficult to control directly this often occurs through control over one's thoughts. Many of the feelings that people have and the reasons they give for them are social and cultural in origin. Acceptable norms for a man in the face of climate change would be to demonstrate being cool, tough or smart.

The emotional impact of climate change is often underestimated. At the deepest level, if one acknowledges global heating and climate change, it can raise feelings of helplessness and power-lessness such that one's sense of identity can feel threatened. I can't manage this! I did not bring children into the world for this! It can make us feel very vulnerable because what helps us to keep going in life is the opposite, feeling that we're safe and secure. Neither should we be surprised these feelings are un-comfortable. This is because they were also the ones we experienced, but could not verbalise, as babies and small children. Am I safe or not safe here? The fact that we couldn't put this into words only made the feelings stronger. It is natural that we want to protect ourselves against things that seem to threaten us. So in relation to climate change people often acknowledge the facts but then deny their importance, as below.

## Everyday denial

*Deny their meaning:* 'I don't think it's that serious.'

*Deny the implications:* 'People have coped with worse in the past. I doubt it will affect us much in the UK.'

*Deny the connections to their own lives:* 'It's not my responsibility - it's down to the government.'

*Deny their emotional significance:* 'I'm not bothered - I've got more important things to worry about.'

*Deny the practical significance:* 'I know it's happening but I can't change my life because of it.'

*Deny the irreversibility:* 'I'm sure it can be sorted out later /we can adapt/ science will find an answer.'

Source: Randall and Brown [3]

Denial seems a pretty good idea in this context. It's not as if we sit down and ask ourselves, 'Shall I deny this information or not?' If at a very deep level the information feels threatening, and I'm not just thinking of climate change here, the doors clang shut instantly. This reaction occurs automatically when we feel suddenly threatened, when danger appears from nowhere. But at some point we need to find the space to reflect on this automatic response. Was I overreacting? Is there something here I can learn about myself if I take a step back for a moment? Denial can be useful - I don't want to acknowledge that my friend is an alcoholic, that this relationship is over, that this is a terminal illness. Denial can save us from pain, but at the expense of avoiding the truth. We tell ourselves stories to buttress denial -

he likes a good drink now and then, deep down she still loves me, I'll get better soon. People give various reasons for denying or being doubtful about climate change, from whether it exists or not to how bad it might be or even whether it's caused by human activity. People argue that no one can see carbon dioxide so global warming can't therefore be happening; that nothing that has happened so far is outside the normal variations of UK weather; that if experts disagree why bother to believe anybody; and that it's a plot by environmentalists to take over the world. The problem with denial though is that it means not really taking responsibility for looking after yourself, your family and friends.

By contrast it's interesting to look at what seems to drive 'professional' sceptics and deniers. These are a small number of people who spend a lot of time and money trying to cast doubt on the findings of climate change scientists. At first this seemed a credible thing to do in the latter part of the twentieth century, as scientist tried different approaches to gain accurate data on global warming and various theories were put forward to explain their findings. There were differing opinions and theories in the scientific community. This, however, is normal. In any area of science ideas are put forward, data obtained, findings checked with others and theories developed, until a consensus occurs as to the likely explanations for a phenomenon. Disagreeing is a vital part of that debate, it is part of the process that scientists use to arrive at a consensus. It doesn't mean, however, that scientists can't be trusted or that science is often wrong.

Some of the tactics that have been used by deniers to attack climate change scientists include the following: alleging there is a conspiracy, that the scientific consensus has arisen through collusion rather than accumulation of evidence; using fake experts to support your story, with credentials that create a facade of respectability; cherry-picking evidence, attacking a point that seems to support your case whilst ignoring everything else; creating impossible standards for your opponents, constantly demanding more evidence; manufacturing doubt, falsely portraying scientists as divided so that acting on their advice would be premature.[4] Until recently such climate change deniers were often given equal space in media events as if their position was equal to that of climate scientists. What this has resulted in is the slowing down of efforts nationally and globally to combat the effects of climate change. Delaying such action through manufacturing doubt has only created more difficult times ahead for us.

Research into the most prominent deniers has found they are often funded by big fossil fuel companies and right-wing think-tanks. This position arises from the belief that any attempt to regulate free-market economics is an attack on human liberty. However, at the heart of such economics is the belief that no government should interfere with the free market, i.e. the right of companies, big and small, to do as they please to make profits for their owners and shareholders. In the US this has meant that legislation to protect the environment has often been attacked or withdrawn in the past. In the US death threats have also been made against leading climate change scientists. Research has shown that in the past such deniers also opposed the scientific evidence on acid rain, the ozone hole and the health dangers associated with smoking.[5] In these cases denial occurs because of strong overriding prior beliefs.

## Psychological impacts

Having looked at why it's difficult to grapple with the realities of climate change and why the denial industry has tried to manu-facture doubt, it is also important to understand how the various impacts of climate change can affect people's health and well-being. This has become a subject of increasing concern and has various elements. One important distinction to make is between sudden disasters caused through climate change and slower gradual effects. Disasters occur at a particular point in time and are highly visible. Floods, hurricanes, bushfires, heat waves and drought are all increasingly in the headlines. Gradual effects, by definition, are much less easy to observe because they build up over time. These include slow changes in average temperatures, sea-level rises, spread of disease, decreased availability of water and increased numbers of displaced people. The impacts will vary accordingly.

Young people in drought-affected areas, for example, have been shown to exhibit high levels of stress and concern about their families. Unsurprisingly, they felt overwhelmed, isolated and worried about the future. A number of people affected by the Hull floods in 2007 were asked to keep diaries for eighteen months to record what happened to them in the aftermath, a period which they often experienced as more traumatic than the flood itself. The diaries highlighted the prolonged impact of this event on families living in temporary accommodation whilst trying to deal with insurers, loss adjusters and builders. Whilst previously local emphasis during periods of floods had been on emergency responses and preparation for disasters this project focused on what happens after disasters. People were encouraged to meet up to share their diaries and it was observed that this process became of crucial importance since it allowed people to share their stories and not to feel so alone. A similar project worked with children and young people to explore how they recovered from flooding using interviews, drawing and workshops. What traumatised young people most was the stress and trauma their parents experienced and all the uncertainty that followed.

A new project on drought in the UK is focusing on seven rivers and their catchment areas. Scientists are producing models of how the availability of water will change as droughts become more frequent. At the same time the experiences, memories and stories of people living in these catchment areas will be recorded to produce a tool for future decision-making. Such a study of drought will be of great value both to the public and to water utilities. With water scarcity becoming more of an issue in the future, for people and environment, such forward-looking studies demonstrate a resourceful preparedness by research councils in funding interdisciplinary teams to support people in potentially threatened areas.

So the psychological impacts of climate change cannot be overlooked, whether it is how people respond to learning about global warming or having had the experience of being flooded out and consequent homelessness. Depending on where you live in the world, if you are lucky you will have a home you can eventually return to, if unlucky you may have no choice but to become a climate refugee.

## Emotional weather

I have sometimes been surprised by the ways in which feelings are often denied in society. I don't just mean troubled feelings, as discussed above, but in some cases the whole spectrum of emotional life. I do have a friend who's quick to point out this is a rather broad generalisation. It is often true in our society that women are left to do the emotional work, by which I mean work which comes directly from the heart and involves being open to feelings, being able to recognise them, name them and express them. It's not that men can't do this but that we've often, but not always, socially and culturally learnt to keep feelings under wraps. It's not that men don't have them, but that they don't necessarily acknowledge them and can tend to express them less often.

It is essential to understand, however, that as human beings we are driven by both head and heart, two sides of the same coin of self. There are times when we can learn most from using our heads and our intellect - observing, describing, analysing, choosing and acting, for example. We all need to be able to do this in our daily lives, whether at home or at work. But we are also creatures that feel and feelings, whether acknowledged or not, inform what we think and believe. Our values come both from what we think *and* feel about different issues. Feelings provide a quite different repertoire of experience. Think of what we can learn about ourselves and others if we are open to feeling fear, love, compassion, grief and solidarity. Knowing about the nature of solidarity is one thing, experiencing it when facing a difficult situation with others is what cements that experience.

When young I was told by someone that I didn't have any feelings. I knew I had them, but it wasn't something I talked about or expressed openly. It took me some time to see that if I didn't talk about my feelings or express them how could anyone know I had them? But what I had learnt as a young boy as part of my socialisation, I realised, was that I was supposed to keep these things to myself. As I came to see, friends welcomed my sharing how I felt and I realised I was reclaiming part of me that had been mislaid. Issues like this affect both our relationships and the way in which we see the world. Not least in relation to climate change we need to be able to name and express both our concerns and our hopes. If we can do this with others we can be much more open in our relationships with friends, family and close others. Given the emotional weather climate change can create, we need to share both how we think and feel with those we want to work with to create change.

But how does one create a space where it feels safe to share one's thoughts and feelings about these matters? Sometimes we just know it's not a good place to do that or alternatively one may be with a friend or friends where it does feel possible. If I can say, 'I do sometimes worry about how climate change may affect my children', it may allow a wider sharing. One could also ask, 'I wonder what others feel about this?' The situation to aim for, if you wish, is to find a few friends who would like to discuss such matters and with whom it feels OK to share. One reason we often don't do this with others is because we assume we will be judged in some way. In any sharing it is useful to agree a few ground rules to create a sense of security in the group as shown below.

## *Helpful ground rules*

*Speaking* - only one person speaks at a time, this can be as a result of agreeing to take it in turns or by putting a hand up.

*Listening* - it is important to listen attentively to what the other person is saying without interrupting them.

*Not judging* - listen without making judgements about the other person respecting where they are coming from.

*Sharing* - no one person should dominate the discussion, no one should be left out, all should be encouraged to contribute.

*Voice* - it's not about saying the right thing or having an answer, it's about finding one's voice, which may just be sharing what one is feeling.

Listening, speaking, sharing, collaborating

Sadly we've often learnt not to share things because we fear negative comment or judgement, often something we learnt in childhood or at school. If I know I can share how I feel with particular others and not be judged this frees me up to be much more open with that person or group of people. I wonder what the people interviewed in that small Norwegian town, referred to earlier, would have shared if they'd felt they had that freedom and trust?

In order to move on it is helpful, if possible, for uncomfortable feelings to be acknowledged and shared in order to thaw out what may have become frozen. In so doing one can begin to feel more safe and hopeful again. The security of working with supportive others is what enables one to move forward. In their book, *Active Hope*, Joanna Macy and Chris Johnstone offer a wealth of ideas for opening up discussion on how one may feel about the world.[6] This can be done in pairs, each individually completing written sentences such as those below (or writing one's own) and sharing them with a partner. For example:

- When I imagine the world we will leave our children, it looks like...
- One of my worst fears about the future is...
- The feelings about this I carry around with me are...
- Some ways I can use these feelings are...

Subsequent discussion will reveal similarities of response as well as differences. From their extensive experience of helping groups work with difficult feelings about the state of the world Macy and Johnstone observe that when fears are brought out into the open they often lose their power to haunt us. It then becomes more possible to tell new stories.

At the same time taking in information about climate change, even in small doses, is challenging and potentially stressful. The Carbon Conversations website is a very useful resource for looking at how groups can learn to talk about issues of sustainability and low-carbon lifestyle in their local community.[7] As well as wise advice on talking with family, friends and colleagues, all sorts of discussion material is available on topics such as energy at home and work, travel and transport, food and water, consumption and waste. The handbook offers down to earth advice and guidance on getting conversations going in the family, with friends, in the workplace and local community. From the above a growing sense of agency can emerge which, in the company of supportive others, can lead to creative action at home and in the locality. This engagement with practical solutions and learning from existing success stories is a major spur for action. From this can come the ability to see a 'new story' that undermines the debilitating trance of global heating.

## Moving forwards

To be able to acknowledge and share troubled feelings with empathetic others does not necessarily remove those feelings, but the opportunity to share them has more power in it than one might imagine. I am reminded of the adage, 'A problem shared is a problem halved.' Knowing and experiencing that others feel in a similar way to you means you aren't alone with those concerns. Energy once used to keep those feelings at bay can now be used for other purposes. If you have a small group of friends or colleagues with this shared concern what might you want to do next with them? It might be to become more aware of other groups and organisations interested in climate issues. And the surprise might be that you are not alone. There will be others in your community, wider area, nationally and globally. One realises one is part of a wider web of connections and this helps bring more focus and energy. There are many others concerned about the hazards of climate change and also how to work towards a more sustainable low-carbon future.

Such work is also vital to the wellbeing of young people as explained here by two experienced educators.

> Teachers need to know how best to help a child 'work through' their worries by acknowledging and verbalising them in a safe and trusting environment. This process of having an adult hear and absorb a child's anxieties (rather than denying or avoiding them) is similar to the early maternal care ... Working through anxieties can

> enable children to take some age appropriate action in relation to their own environment, providing a sense of agency and control to mitigate anxious feelings about powerlessness and helplessness. It also helps children to develop their critical thinking capacity.[8]

The above are all steps in developing a sense of agency, that is the feeling that with like-minded others one can begin to make a difference. From here on this is what the book is about. You have acquired basic information about the significance of climate matters, fossil fuels and the need for a low-carbon future. There is more one can learn if one chooses and the notes and references at the end of this book are designed to help you in this. Identifying examples of existing low-carbon change and visiting them with others, whether in people's homes, the local community or farther afield, can be inspirational. One can begin to put some of the bits together in the mind's eye and gradually build a picture of how things are changing and how they need to change. This is about developing your own vision, with others, of where you feel you need to get to. Having a clear vision is like a guiding star always there to draw us onwards. See also chapter 7.

The American Psychological Association comments as follows.

> Individual's perceptions that effective collective action on climate change is possible may be even more important than their beliefs about effective individual action... Providing a forum where people can share what they are doing, and learn about what others are doing can lead to a positive feedback loop in which actions inspire other actions and support the creation of new social norms.[9]

At the heart of this is connecting with like-minded and supportive others. It is also important to cultivate hope. The word hope gets used in all sorts of different ways from the mundane to the profound. Hoping that I will not miss the last post for a letter is important to me but doesn't signify much in the wider scheme of things. I hope the sun will shine tomorrow and that I will see my grandchildren next week. This is, if you like, an everyday use of the word 'hope'. But hope has much more to offer than this.

What I am interested in here is what one might call authentic or active hope, the hope that is needed when the going gets tough, when we are seriously running out of options. It is the sort of hope that keeps us going in the most difficult of times. Hope gives us the strength to go on in such times and draws on a variety of powerful sources. It is also true that such hope does not necessarily mean one will achieve one's goal. Some of the sources people have shared with me are briefly described here.

## *Sources of hope*

- *The natural world* ~ a source of beauty, wonder and inspiration which ever renews itself and ever refreshes the heart and mind.
- *Other people's lives* ~ the way in which both ordinary and extraordinary people manage difficult life situations with dignity.
- *Collective struggles* ~ groups in the past and the present which have fought to achieve the equality and justice that is rightfully theirs.
- *Visionaries* ~ those who offer visions of an earth transformed and who work to help to bring this about in different ways.
- *Faith and belief* ~ which may be spiritual or political and which offers a framework of meaning in both good times and bad.
- *Human creativity* ~ the constant awe-inspiring upwelling of music, poetry, and the arts, an essential element of the human condition.
- *Mentors and colleagues* ~ at work and at home who offer inspiration by their deeds and encouragement with their words.
- *Relationships* ~ the being loved by partners, friends and family that nourishes and sustains us in our lives.
- *Humour* ~ seeing the funny side of things, being able to laugh in adversity, having fun, celebrating together.

Source: Author[10]

I wonder which catch your attention and which you can relate to from your own experience? It is worth remembering the ancient Greek story of Pandora. When she opened the box which contained in it all the troubles of the world they suddenly flew free and, last of all, hope also flew out. So what one might therefore call authentic hope can be a vital source of strength in turbulent times, the power to continue, to believe one can make a difference, to change things for the better.[11] The choice to be faced is between getting stranded in fear and denial on the one hand or choosing to work with others to help create more sustainable low-carbon communities.

# Part Three

**Working for change**

# 7. Getting things done

*For a new generation to realise a new vision of citizenship as mutual interdependence on a finite planet, we will need many sites of struggle and conversation which connect to foster new narratives of collaboration and community.*

- Bronwyn Hayward, writer on citizenship[1]

This chapter explores some of the things which encourage us to be active in the world and looks at why this skill may be developed or neglected as we are growing up. Wanting to be active in changing things for the better in the face of global warming may not seem at all easy. In this context it is useful to explore the importance of emotional wellbeing, the ability to empathise with others and the need to deepen our appreciation of the natural world. The latter part of this chapter includes inspiring examples of action for change at the grassroots level. For reasons already referred to in chapter 4 we know it can be difficult to talk about climate change because of unwritten social taboos and, given its breadth and complexity, because it at first seems difficult to act on. Being involved in action for change on one's own may be a scary business, especially if it is about challenging the status quo. But working with others to change things for the better in one's community can also be an empowering experience - the impact is more than would be the case if one was just working on one's own.

## A sense of agency

The importance of developing a sense of agency was mentioned in chapter 4. It is a term one might have come across in the context of child development, education or psychology. In these contexts it means the awareness that one is able to change things, whether a small child realising they can affect their mother's behaviour or a group of climate activists understanding what needs to be done to achieve a particular goal. So how does one develop a sense of agency, the belief that one can change things in a way that one wishes? The opposite of course is the sense that whatever one does to change things it doesn't make any difference. This could be in the context of a relationship, a family, at work or in daily life. It could be in relation to quite big things or quite small ones. So it really does make a difference if one feels one has the power to change situations or not. Some things will be easier to change than others, one may thus have a sense of agency in particular areas of life but not in another. And, of course, the crunch is that initially it may not be easy to have a sense of agency in the face of big issues such as changing climate.

A sense of agency is an important part of being human. It is one of the many aspects of identity that emerges from our childhood experiences and our education, whether formal or informal. It is an area well understood by many parents and teachers of younger children, although perhaps not all. Whilst we begin life completely dependent and needing protection childhood is essentially about our journey into independence and standing on our own two feet. Early on we begin to get a sense of ourselves as individuals, wanting to know more about our surroundings and how to control things. We begin to develop our skills and know what we like and dislike. An important part of gaining this independence is the realisation that we are part of a community, whether at home, playgroup or in school. We need to learn how to relate to others as well as going for what we individually want in different situations. Learning about the need to react respon-sibly towards others is a constant reminder that we are members of a larger community. It is through these processes of everyday action and learning that we develop a sense of achievement and responsibility.

In so doing children learn confidence in exploring the world, asking questions and making decisions. This doesn't mean that everything goes smoothly or easily for we also need to learn how to negotiate, face up to difficulties and deal with failure. It is as important to learn from one's failures as one's successes. In discussion with my students I noticed one of their major fears was 'making a mistake'. This was something to be hidden away and preferably not brought out into the open where it might cause acute embarrassment. When asked where this notion came from they often cited what teachers had said to them at school. I suggested an alternative view, based on the process of film making, where a scene might be shot several times before the actors get it just as the director wants. Something was learnt from each 'take' until their performance was the best it could be. A mis-take, I suggested, should rather be seen as a valuable step in the learning process. Belittling or derision is unhelpful and not appropriate in any sort of learning context. It may require several takes before one gets things just right.

Offering children choices in different situations allows them to develop confidence in their own decision-making skills. Childhood and education are about gradually widening those choices, developing new skills and becoming ready to have a say on matters around one. Listening respectfully to young people's views and opinions encourages their sense of agency, allows them to check things out and make tentative or bold steps to see what they can achieve. This is why discussion and debate provide such important forums for growth and the honing of social skills. It is also why such occasions require respectful ground rules so that everyone's views are listened to attentively, even if they are not one's own (chapter 6).

## Emotional well-being

Developing a healthy sense of agency is one of the key skills needed if one wants to effect change in today's rapidly changing world. Graham Music, in his book *The Good Life*, identifies what many have observed about the changing quality of life over recent decades.

I am thinking about what prominent sociologists have described about life becoming faster and harsher, with less continuity and security, with community and mutual support seemingly waning, and the individual increasingly deemed more important than the group. Allied to this we have seen an increasing emphasis on material consumption, on status, fame and its symbols. Many have also made a link between business methods, financial practices geared to profit irrespective of human costs, and a lack of concern for the planet's ecosystems.[2]

This is the backdrop against which we have to face the varied issues presented to us by changing climate. What sort of qualities do we and young people need to have in order to cope with changes that lie ahead? In such times we need competent, confident adults and young people more than ever before. It is important, therefore, to be aware of the wider context of social development and the ways in which this affects how we learn to relate to other people and also to the natural world. We can learn to be caring towards others and nature or deny the humanity of others and ignore the role of nature (the biosphere) in our lives. The three threads I want to highlight here are caring for others, working cooperatively with others and caring for the environment. Each is an essential element in what it means to be human and each can be nurtured and nourished or denied and trampled on.

As an example of how we are primed to be helpful and supportive from a very early age Music cites an experiment with fifteen-month-old toddlers. In this an adult takes some books and puts them in a cupboard but when she goes back for more books the door closes. On returning she doesn't have a free hand with which to open the cupboard. As soon as they see her predicament the toddlers always get up to open the door. They do this without any ulterior motive just wanting to help when they see someone has a problem. Many other experiments have shown this desire to help others as being present from a very early age. This urge to help is an example of empathy at work which is the ability to put oneself in someone else's shoes - observing the situation someone else may be in, not just through one's own eyes but through the other person's eyes. As one gets older one becomes more aware of what someone else is likely to be feeling, whether hurt, embarrassment or delight, and one can resonate with this. As a result one is likely to support, intervene or protect the other person as seems appropriate, because you and she experience similar things and have similar feelings. One can, of course, also learn not to be helpful and not to be empathetic. If these qualities were devalued in childhood or if one's own hurt in life is too big to manage one may enjoy not helping someone out (if you were never helped) and not empathising (if no one ever empathised with you).

## Nature and nurture

How and whether one feels a direct relationship with the natural environment is often seen as a matter of individual choice and something which doesn't have any particular consequence for oneself or others. Growing up in a city can sometimes limit one's experience of open and wild places, although a visit to such can also lead to a lifelong love affair. Research shows that humans have a natural affinity with open spaces, seashore, woodland, rivers and mountains, but importantly this also can be either nourished or ignored when young. I referred in chapter 3 to a time when I worked with students who were training to be primary teachers and quizzed them about their sense of awe and wonder in relationship to the natural world. Their silence and discomfort then turned out to be because this was not something one normally spoke about. When I gave them permission to do this, to revisit their early memories, they were there for instant recall as they spoke of dew on grass, jumping in puddles, frost on windows, flowers as tall as themselves, watching waves on a beach, the view from a hill. They remembered and connected with their own filed away and nearly forgotten feelings of awe and wonder. It is feelings like these which both nurture us and make us want to care for and protect the world.

Unless children spend time in the great outdoors
how will they ever come to love and protect the natural world?

If children or adults have little interest in or experience of the natural environment they are unlikely to be concerned about their own impact or the impact of others on it, let alone understand its role as our life-support system. It's really important that young people and adults learn from and in turn learn how to care for the natural world in different ways. Some of the ways in which this can be encouraged are set out below.

## *Nurture in the environment*

1.  Take young people to spend time in the natural environment, whether parks, fields, woods, hills, lakes or at the coast.

2.  Help young people find something positive to do in the natural environment, whether looking after a place, growing things, appreciating it through study, drawing or playing there.

3.  Listen seriously to concerns young people may have about the natural world and encourage them to tell you how they feel about places.

4. Find out what they know, what they think they know and what they'd like to know about the places they go to.

5. Reassure children in relation to their concerns and help them develop a sense of agency here, a willingness to participate in care of the environment.

Playing, exploring, learning, enjoying, looking after, being listened to and supported, all of these directly and indirectly help develop a respect for and love of different natural environments. If it is true that we only protect that which we love, such experiential learning will help young people and adults feel a greater connection with, and responsibility for, the biosphere, and thus be prepared to fight for its protection. In what other context would we ignore or damage a life-support system on which our very existence depended?

## Working together

In the individualistic world we now live in (see Graham Music above), it may seem a bit much to try and 'save the world', as the old slogan went, and no wonder because no one person could achieve that. Things change when people work collaboratively together with others to achieve a particular goal for, as systems thinking or ecological thinking tells us, the sum is always more than the parts. In part citizenship is about the obligations people may owe to society although notions of citizenship vary over historical time and in different cultural contexts. In the western world two broad but differing traditions can be identified: the 'liberal tradition' in which citizenship is seen as being about the protection of the individual's rights and the 'republican tradition' which focuses on the responsibilities and duties that each individual owes to the community to ensure its smooth and fair functioning.

Bronwyn Hayward's work with young people on their ideas about citizenship is both revealing and challenging here. While my own notion of citizenship is that of people working collaboratively together to achieve a common end this was not a very common idea amongst the young people she talked to. She found, for example, that individualism and competition are encouraged much more than a sense of obligation to others or an emphasis on the common good. She noted widespread unease that children now equate 'good citizenship' with habits of individual responsibility and ethical consumption which leave the underlying causes of environmental and social problems unchallenged.[3]

Hayward goes on to elaborate on the wider and deeper forms of agency that are needed for citizens, organisations and governments to face both present dilemmas and those that lie ahead. Piecemeal efforts and scratching the surface will not be enough as neither was the rearranging of deckchairs on the Titanic. Any attempts at change which fail to recognise the power and grip of the old high-carbon story will be valueless in the face of the challenge before us. As Naomi Klein clearly illustrates in *This Changes Everything*, a high-carbon view of citizenship is the worst not the best way forward.[4] What one needs to be able to imagine today is what an equally powerful sense of agency looks like when directed towards ecologically sustainable, socially just and low-carbon ends.

In this chapter I have talked about both adults and young people because they are equally important in these times. Indeed, we can talk of the older generation, the present generation and the younger generation, all of whom can unknowingly contribute to climate change or who can knowingly adapt to the changes that are beginning to occur and work to mitigate some of the impacts. The older generation unwittingly helped create global warming because they were brought up on the old high-carbon story. It is also important to recall that a good number of the older generation recognised the emerging environmental problems back in the 70s and 80s when they were young and worked to help resolve these (see chapter 6). Members of the present generation were also probably brought up on the high-carbon story as many economists and politicians insist on the need to privatise, i.e. sell off, all aspects of society in a way which consumes the earth's resources with little thought for tomorrow. What then of the younger generation, those who will inherit a tricky tomorrow?

It does matter what each generation thinks and feels about the present and future because it will influence the tomorrow they help create. We have a responsibility, I would argue, not only to our own generation, but also to those who will come after us, children, grandchildren and those as yet unborn. We share a responsibility not just across space (local to global) but also across time. I was interested therefore to come across a report setting out what a sample of today's teenagers see as their responsibilities, entitled 'Today's teenagers are more engaged with social issues than ever...'

The report shows the true face of the next generation. On just about every indicator, the popular stereotypes are wrong. Today's teenagers are shown to be behaving more responsibly when it comes to drink and drugs; caring more about social issues both at home and abroad; and being more willing to get out and take action to make their world a better place.

> Critically, the report reveals that teenagers and their teachers want more opportunities for young people to engage in social action. Both groups recognise the profound impact that social action can have in terms of skills for life and work - confidence, wellbeing, teamwork and leadership.[5]

Those who study the characteristics of different generations note that a new generation emerges every 15 to 20 years. This study reports on a sample of those between the ages of 14 and 17 which they called 'Generation Citizen'. Their main findings are below.

### *Generation Citizen*

1. Today's teenagers are more engaged with social issues both globally and locally than previous generations of teenagers.

2. Teenagers see themselves as less engaged with traditional politics than previous generations of teenagers and teachers agree.

3. Teenagers see charities and social enterprises, alongside personal volunteering and social action, as the most important agents for positive change in their local communities.

4. Today's teenagers are highly active through volunteering and other forms of social action.

5. Teenagers who volunteered reported higher levels of wellbeing, social cohesion and employability.

6. Although teenagers prefer real world engagement in their communities, teenagers are increasingly using social media for social action.

7. Getting a job, living costs and bullying concern teenagers the most.

8. Teenagers see negative media portrayals as having a detrimental impact on their lives and future.

9. Teenagers desire careers that change the world for the better and help people less fortunate and the majority are ethical consumers.

10. British teenagers cite inspirational leaders and celebrities who use their fame for positive action as role models.

Source: Birdwell and Bani[6]

This sample is taken from 14-17 year olds who chose to be involved in volunteering work. Not all those in this age group may wish to do this but it is becoming increasingly popular as an important and valuable social skill. The survey findings are thus representative of a segment of this generation which, given their interest in active citizenship, has been labelled in this study as 'Generation Citizen'. In the work that needs to be done in relation to climate change there are important links that can be made across the generations and an even more powerful sense of cross-generational agency developed.

There are many examples of such a sensibility at work today in relation to climate change and the need to create more sustainable local communities. The three illustrative examples below are taken from the Carbon Conversations Programme, the Transition Network and the practice of Flatpack Democracy.

## CASE STUDY - Carbon Conversations

Carbon Conversations is a programme which facilitates small community discussion groups over a period of 3-6 months to explore and reduce the impact of their carbon footprint and trains and supports volunteer facilitators across the UK. The package includes a detailed handbook, *In Time for Tomorrow*, written by psychotherapist and group facilitator Rosemary Randall and Andy Brown, an engineer with a background in social sciences.[7] Their combination of a trained facilitator, a small group and in-depth discussion over several months develops a strong sense of agency in relation to working for change. Here is how one participant reported on what he subsequently did.

### Upgrading a 1960s house

Our house was built in 1968. I've lived there since 1996 with my wife and two children who are now teenagers. When we first moved here I was too busy with full-time work and a young family to do much but more recently I realised that our home was overflowing with stuff and that we could do a lot to lead a more environmental life. I first became interested in environmental issues in my twenties, both because of the connection with a more spiritual and pacifist outlook and for the social connections that came from being part of a group.

A 1960s house may look quite modern but most of them need a lot of upgrades. We started by insulating both under the rafters and under the boarding between the joists. The next thing was dealing with the central heating. We upgraded to a condensing boiler, put thermostatic radiator valves on all the radiators and installed new controls. All our lighting is low-energy and we've gradually replaced most of our appliances with the most efficient ones. We replaced the windows with uPVC double glazed units and finally installed photovoltaic panels three years ago.

Since starting the work I have bought a thermometer for the house so we can see exactly what the temperature is and it's made me more likely to put on warmer clothes than turn up the heating. As well as upgrading the house, we have bought a hybrid car, eat less meat and installed water butts in the garden.

We didn't make an overall plan but we did take advantage of grants as they became available and so that drove some of our decisions. We did the work gradually, over a ten year period and spent about £26,000 on it. It is important to me to know that we are doing the right things for the environment. We have hosted two Superhomes open days, and I think the visitors were interested and motivated by seeing what we've done.

The most rewarding aspect is knowing we are using clean renewable energy when the sun is shining.

Source: Randall and Brown[8]

## CASE STUDY - Transition Network

This is an international network of well over a thousand neighbourhoods, villages, towns and cities across the world, committed to the transition towards a more sustainable low-carbon way of living. Different communities focus on different aspects of this, from energy, food and transport to housing, waste and education. The different emphases reflect both the interests of those who set up the initial group and also the particular issues for that community. These initiatives emerge at a grassroots level and illustrate what different aspects of such a transition could look like. They are designed to encourage, inspire and enact the changes that need to come about to make local communities more resilient in the face of economic hardship, rising energy prices and ongoing carbon emissions. These projects also model different ways of being and more sustainable ways of going forward. The Transition Network is a lively, interactive, multifaceted response to the many issues raised by the unsustainable high-carbon story. It works to demonstrate how the transition can be made away from the high-carbon story and towards a more localised low-carbon story.

### The rise of community energy

Energy generation is something done by huge energy companies, right? Wrong. Community energy is one of the key ways communities can start to take back control of their economy, and their energy supply.

### Context

Around the world, the idea that communities install, own, and enjoy some of the benefits of renewable energy is growing fast. In Germany over 50 percent of renewable energy being installed is in community ownership. In the UK alone, over 5000 community groups have set up community energy schemes since 2008. Many of these have been Transition groups, and the schemes they have come up with have varied widely in terms of size.

### Why it matters

This surge in community energy projects is a powerful story. They offer the potential for greater democratic control, for shared benefits and for greater active participation of the community which can, in turn, lead to infrastructure and cultural change. Decarbonising our energy system requires decentralised renewables, which lead us to far greater opportunities for community investment and involvement. And it brings people together, and creates opportunities for conversation, for parties, for relationships. And it's change people can see happening around them, which means the changes we need to make don't seem so far off and impossible.

**Brixton Energy**

This grew out of Transition Town Brixton and has: i) installed 134.24 kW of solar energy across three schemes; ii) raised a total investment of £182,000 from local people through three share offers; iii) saved around 1,275 tons of CO2; iv) benefitted from 290 hours of volunteer input.

They are currently planning Brixton Energy 4, bringing the electricity (solar-generated!) back to Electric Avenue, one of the area's best-known streets. Mary Simpson, who has lived in Brixton Hill for 26 years, commented 'This project means a lot to us and our residents as it brings with it valuable work experience for some of our youth as well as an investment opportunity for residents and local investors alike'.

Source: Hopkins[9]

## CASE STUDY - Flatpack Democracy

This account of a new approach to politics is described as 'the story of what happened and an instruction manual for taking political power at a local level, then using it to enable people to have a greater say in the decisions that affect their lives'. It is based on what happened in the small market town of Frome in Somerset.[9] As in many other towns the local council reflected party politics in a divisive way which often overrode local interests and needs. However, a group which called itself Independents for Frome (IfF) set out to challenge what they felt was an outdated and unhelpful status quo.

### *Independents for Frome*

In our experience, at local levels of representation, party politics as practised by the current political parties are an irrelevant and corrosive diversion. A diversion which critically reduces the pool of people prepared to serve as councillors. The people who formed Independents for Frome (IfF) came together because they cared about their local community and wished to focus solely on bringing benefits to Frome. We developed a Way of Working which is not simply to form another party. Our intention was not to replace one set of individuals struggling within the system with another, but to try and invent a process that would drag local decision making into the 21st century. Within IfF we maintain that 'Yes' is a better answer than 'No'; that the possibility of making mistakes should be encouraged; that diversity and different views are positive; and that community leadership is about making bold, local decisions.

What we are trying to do in Frome is attempting to create a new, inclusive democracy, starting from the grassroots up. We've only just begun this process and have succeeded in only some areas. As far as possible, this guide draws on parallel experiences taking place in other parts of the country.

Source: Macfadyen[10]

In setting up Independents for Frome the group wanted to radically challenge the face of local politics and set out to have an Independent candidate standing in all the seats. When election-day came IfF won ten of the seventeen seats. It was time for a new beginning. They agreed on five essential ingredients which they felt underpinned what they called the 'Frome Model'. These were: 1. Work together as a group; 2. Agree your ways of working together; 3. You can't do this alone - use facilitators, friends, experts, people with skills; 4. Keep it light; 5. Identify a good name for the new group. They also identified areas they could all agree on as important. Under Environment these included promoting a cleaner/greener Frome; planting more trees on public land; liaising with community groups; expanding the provision of allotments. IfF thus began to revolutionise both the process of local politics (more participatory and less nonconfrontational) as well as the focus (sustainability as the central plank).

It would seem that when local resilience is identified as a key theme in the community all sorts of interesting things begin to happen. People take a particular interest in what is happening in their own locality and in enhancing local resilience and wellbeing. Creating a more thriving and sustainable community enhances local democracy, inventiveness and ingenuity. With the future of one's community at stake, in a whole variety of ways, greater engagement becomes both necessary and liberating.

# 8. Adapting to climate change

*By failing to prepare, you are preparing to fail.*

- Benjamin Franklin, Founding Father of the United States[1]

As the opening chapter made clear climate change has already begun to affect the weather that people experience across the globe. What this looks like varies but, because warmer air holds more moisture, it is becoming more volatile than before and therefore more unstable and unpredictable. This is different from the variations in weather we traditionally like to talk about in the UK. For some considerable time now climate scientists across the world have predicted that extreme weather events will occur more often, whether drought and wildfires, flooding and sea-level rise, freezing winters or storms and hurricanes. In the UK it is likely that stronger storms and floods, heat waves and drought as well as really cold winters, will increasingly become more common. Whilst it's not yet known just how frequent these events will be they are part of our new norm. Since weather extremes impact on all aspects of daily life - from homes, travel and work to food, communications and safety - it would seem prudent to be prepared for such new situations. This chapter firstly looks at adapting to the safety aspects of more extreme weather and secondly adapting to other fundamental changes in different aspects of daily life.

A recent UK poll showed that 64 percent of people saw global warming as a problem now and 70 percent felt it would be in twenty years' time. Flooding and sea-level rise were the highest climate concerns amongst respondents whilst more than half were worried about droughts and water shortages.[2] It is no surprise then that Britons are concerned about how they can adapt to climate change. Adapting to climate change means not being caught out when such events occur, it means knowing what to do and how to adapt one's life and community so that loved ones and neighbours are safe. Being prepared means both being safer than one might otherwise have been and adapting in advance to changing conditions that one might not have hitherto foreseen.

Make no mistake, at some time or other we are all likely to face extremes of weather that we have not experienced before. This will happen because of the amount of greenhouse gases already in the atmosphere, let alone the emissions we are still creating. Whilst in the past common sense may have seen us through we now need to be more alert and prepared for weather hazards which will be of a different order. The first part of this chapter considers questions such as, 'What do I need to be prepared for?' and 'What do I need to do to stay safe?' In particular it looks at some of the adaptations in lifestyle that will need to be made in the face of stormier weather - increasing flooding and sea level rise - as well as higher temperatures, more frequent heatwaves and drought. Whilst official sources on these hazards go into some detail on what needs to be done in order to stay safe, this chapter provides an introduction to the changing scene as well as examples of how daily life in home and community more generally will need to adapt in the face of global heating.

Most people don't go looking for emergency advice on Government websites until disaster is imminent, but by then the advice may be too late. In such situations people often leave things until it's too late because they can't imagine flooding, for example, happening in their area. It hasn't in the past so why should it now? Or it happens so suddenly that there is no time to prepare. In Cumbria in 2009 the floodwater at Cockermouth was nearly a meter deep in the main street and the winter flooding of the Somerset Levels in 2013-14 covered nearly 7000 hectares of countryside. In 2015 parts of Cumbria were flooded badly again. It is perhaps only when one has experienced such traumas that one fully understands the need for emergency planning. However, I have to admit, I had not actually given much thought to these matters until I began researching this chapter.

Whilst adults have a longer timescale against which to assess changes in the weather it is important to remember that the weather we grew up with as children became our norm. Weather which adults may see as different or extreme will not necessarily be experienced as such by young people, it will become their norm. We have a responsibility, however, to ourselves and young people to be prepared for torrential rain, unexpected flooding and periodic drought. This includes protection of buildings, having appropriate clothing and having agreed safety rules. For children a sense of 'normality' is important - this is what we do in these circumstances, this is why it's important. For smaller children it can be like a game rather than something that causes alarm. Here, therefore, I look at some of the things that can be done to adapt to increasingly stormy weather, flooding and drought, all of which are predicted to occur increasingly in the UK.

## Increased flooding

I mentioned previously a newspaper headline which read, 'Now climate experts warn that every house in the country is at risk of flooding.' I thought this couldn't be true, as not all houses are near a river. What the article stressed, however, was that given the increasingly torrential nature of rain, one didn't need to be near a river to be in danger, as flooding can also occur when road gullies, sewers and drainage ditches become overwhelmed by heavy rain, so there is no home safe from that risk. Whilst the emphasis here is on safety at home one might equally be somewhere else or on the way to or from work.

Flooding can come in various forms, from winter storms when land may already be saturated and summer storms when the ground is baked by drought. There are four main sources of flooding - tidal, coming from the sea and rivers; as a result of rivers bursting their banks; groundwater flooding, when the earth is saturated by rain; flash flooding, when drainage systems are overwhelmed. It is important to know which of these sources is likely to threaten your home. Are you likely to get floods in your area or places that you visit? You can get useful advice about this in the UK from the flood maps on the Environmental Agency's website.[3] It has to be said that the floodplain of a river is not the best place to live, although property developers and builders have traditionally ignored the danger signified by this label in their eagerness to make a profit.

Whilst this chapter does not aim to provide a comprehensive review of advice on flood planning it does highlight some of the key issues that householders need to note and some useful sources of information on this.[4] Advice on flooding generally covers three main areas: prior preparation and planning before it happens; what to do during a period of flood; recovering and cleaning up after a flood. It is important to know whether flood warning messages are available in your area or not and to understand what different warnings mean. This runs from flood alert (be prepared for possible flooding) to flood warning (flooding expected, immediate action required) and severe flood warning (danger to life). Is your property insured against flooding? What items do you need to have with you if you need to exit quickly from the building? In the commotion that may occur remember to switch off electricity/water/gas before the water gets in. Floodwater is also likely to be contaminated water. Other things to definitely *not* do are going to see where the flood is occurring, especially near rivers; walking through floodwater, as six inches of fast flowing water can knock a person over; driving through floodwater, as two feet of water can float a car; trying to swim in fast flowing water, as one may get swept away or struck by an object and walking by river banks or bridges, as in extreme situations they can collapse.[5]

There is also work that can be done in one's immediate area to minimise the impact of flooding. This is clearing out of drains and drainage ditches, planting trees to slow run-off on slopes and not putting down paving, brickwork or tarmac since they prevent rain or floodwater from draining away. It is also important to safeguard buildings from the outside, checking what sort of barriers and protection can help reduce flood water coming into the home, whether through airbricks, doors or windows. Flood waters can rise quickly so any prepared barriers need to be quick to fit. The Blue Pages are a useful source of information in preparing for such situations.[6] Perhaps the observations made here seem alarmist on the one hand or alternatively such common sense they don't need highlighting. My sense is that, unless proved otherwise, we often don't expect such things to happen to us.

## Higher temperatures

It may seem a jump from floods to heatwaves and drought but nevertheless, according to the Environment Agency, both are likely to become more common as a result of climate change. They're going to be part of our new norm, as in 2012 when weather in the UK went from record levels of drought to some of the worst flooding ever. Both local communities and national organisations will increasingly need to be prepared for such events. In terms of drought management farmers need to be encouraged to create their own reservoirs and water companies may not be allowed to abstract water from rivers indefinitely. A small localised drought is easier to deal with because water can be moved from one place to another but it is an entirely different matter if it involves a whole region. We will therefore increasingly have to adapt to issues of water management, whether in the home, on the farm or in an industrial context. UK droughts are expected to be more severe and to affect larger areas of the country. The intense heatwave in Russia in 2010 saw 50,000 people die.

So what do we need to know in order to adapt our lifestyles and homes to stay fit and healthy in a long heat wave? We love warm and sunny weather and indeed its onset can bring much pleasure and relief. As I heard someone exclaim recently, 'Ah, at last we're benefiting from the fruits of global warming!' However, the thing about our changing weather, our new norm, is that such conditions can turn into a heatwave and even drought. Short heatwaves may be enjoyable but a long heatwave brings health risks for young and old and, in particular, can make heart and breathing problems worse. As the Met Office highlights, 'Extreme heat can force the body into overdrive as it tries to stay cool through perspiration and evaporation. Young children and older people are particularly at risk. Overexposure to sun is equally dangerous, with effects ranging from mild sunburn to skin cancer. It doesn't have to be hot for the UV (ultraviolet) index to be high.' [7] Extreme heat is a particular threat to health and heat-related deaths are expected to increase dramatically over the years ahead.

Some of the advice on what to do may seem obvious but it's important to remember that high temperatures are especially dangerous for the elderly, the very young, and those with chronic or long-term medical conditions, such as a heart condition or breathing problems. As with flooding there will be media alerts and, given the temperatures it is best to avoid unnecessary travel and keep an eye on those who are older or vulnerable. The coolest room is the best place to be. Shutters or reflective material outside the windows can help keep the room cool whilst dark curtains and metal blinds will make rooms hotter. Whilst the room is cooler than it is outside its best to keep windows closed but open at night if the air outside is cooler. As someone who finds real heat difficult anyway I learnt long ago to avoid going out between 11.00 and 3.00, the hottest part of the day. Look for shade, plant more trees in streets and gardens. Drink water or fruit juice but avoid tea, coffee and alcohol (yes that could be hard), take a lukewarm shower. Symptoms of heat exhaustion include headaches, dizziness, nausea and vomiting, muscle weakness or cramps, pale skin, high temperature. Heatstroke can occur if heat exhaustion is left untreated but can also occur without warning.[8]

Whilst various national agencies have guidelines online it doesn't necessarily mean members of the public are aware of them or would necessarily follow them. Neither does it mean that government departments, advisory bodies and support agencies have all the necessary procedures in place. It has been observed that there are a number of ways in which the UK is underprepared for heatwaves.[9] For example, many modern flats have windows pointing only in one direction, which means one can't create a draught or cross-ventilation. Homes in North Africa or the Middle East, by contrast, are often based around a central courtyard where air flow can create cool places. Very few houses in the UK have air conditioning, but in America this accounts for 15 percent of extra energy consumption. Rail tracks can expand in extreme heat and road surfaces melt. In the US ad hoc 'cooling centres' are set aside, air-conditioned public buildings (community centres or libraries) offer relief from the heat. Another US idea is to extend the opening hours of public swimming pools. More shaded outdoor seating is also needed, as found in France, together with public drinking fountains.

When heatwaves become serious they can often merge into drought. In the UK we are used to thinking of droughts as something that happen elsewhere in the world and often in poorer areas. This is yet another stereotype as droughts can equally occur in industrialised countries. Severe droughts occur naturally in many parts of the world as a result of traditional climatic conditions. However, global warming can make such droughts last even longer and with profound social and economic implications. From 1997 to 2009 Australia faced the worst drought in the country's history. In Melbourne, a city of 4.3 million people, water reserves dropped to an all-time low of 25 per cent. But the city also reduced its water demand per head by almost 50 per cent as the result of numerous water conservation programmes, from domestic rainwater holding tanks to bans on watering lawns and washing cars. Water-saving appliances reduced household water use from 85 to 55 gallons per person. These savings were the result of concerted effort at both government and local levels. Water is one of the most taken-for-granted resources in industrialised countries and consequently a resource which is often wasted on a grand scale. A new ethic of water conservation in home and community will be part of the wider adaptation process that we will all need to make in the face of increasing heatwaves and drought.

In the UK an interdisciplinary team has been brought together to explore the impact of drought on seven rivers and their catchment areas across the country.[10] Scientists plan to produce detailed models of how water availability is likely to change as droughts become more frequent in the country, a good example of how present research can be beneficial in the future - forewarned is forearmed. As well as scientific data researchers will also collect other types of knowledge - experiences, memories and stories of people who live in the seven catchment areas. The project engages with both the need for more detailed scientific knowledge on drought as well as the experiences and personal knowledge held within the local communities.

## Rising sea levels

Sea levels have begun to rise around the world because a warming ocean is an expanding one. A new and more detailed way of measuring these changes has recently shown that global sea levels have risen faster than previously thought over the last century. This suggests climate change is having a bigger-than-expected impact on sea level rise. The consequences of this are far reaching given the number of world cities that lie in coastal areas or just above sea level. Our fossil fuel driven civilisation will create a profoundly altered planet and one to which we will necessarily have to adapt. Low-lying coastal areas will become inundated and the reach of storm surges extended. Gradually urban authorities around the world are beginning to recognise the scope of the problem and the multiple responsibilities involved.

One of the different responses occurring in relation to adaptation to sea level rise is that between 'hard' and 'soft' solutions. Traditionally in the twentieth century engineering was seen as offering the best solutions to encroaching seas (and control of rivers) with dikes, seawalls and dams built to keep rising waters at bay. It is now widely recognised that this confrontational approach to controlling natural processes, such as tidal flows and meandering rivers, can over a period of time make things worse. These natural processes have a vital part to play, as in the creation and extension of wetlands, marshes and mudflats that soak up excess water and can help protect other areas. Earlier methods, which focused on trying to control nature, are now seen as creating another layer of problems down the line, whereas working with and through natural systems provides much greater resilience.

Some areas of the UK, such as Yorkshire's Holderness coast and parts of the Norfolk coast, have long been subject to erosion by the sea. Towns such as Skegness and Great Yarmouth have been identified as at particular risk from sea level rise. Soft, easily eroded cliffs, can collapse dramatically in the face of existing storm surges let alone those arising from higher sea level. Over the years some rural communities in Norfolk have seen houses collapsing and falling to the beach below. Local residents have been shocked at the lack of help or compensation from local and national authorities. In the UK, however, the Coastal Protection Act of 1949 is quite clear - governments do not compensate house owners for properties lost to the sea. In 2009, a trial programme offered £11 million to help coastal communities adapt rather than build further flood defences. Adapting, in this case, meant moving further inland. Few residents took up this option because the price offered by the council was insufficient to take up the option of rebuild.

Whilst local authorities have to produce their own flood plans there are many other important initiatives focusing on flooding and sea-level change. One such is 'Living with a Changing Coast', a cross-channel project aimed at helping coastal communities to better understand and prepare for impacts of climate change, especially in relation to sea-level rise and coastal erosion.[11] The Exe Estuary and Poole Harbour are the English locations, with five different French locations - Veys Bay, Sienne Havre, Saire Valley, Saane Valley and Orne Estuary, all on the Normandy coast. Poole and the Orne Estuary are both major ferry terminals, the Exe, Sienne Havre and Veys Bay all internationally important sites for wading birds. In terms of managing the coastal environment the main issues are loss of wetlands, the future of farming and infrastructure, flood management, tourism and the economy.

Businesses, communities, local authorities and government all have a crucial role to play in these matters. The project notes that to adapt to coastal change we need to:

- Understand how the coast might change in the future
- Understand what the positive and negative impacts of this change might be
- Consider our options for minimising the negative impacts and taking advantage of opportunities
- Choose the preferred options and secure funding
- Implement the options [12]

Working with local organisations and groups embraces those who will be directly affected by sea level changes in the area and considering their concerns for the future. Through this process the project is creating a rich resource bank of information gathered from both experts and local people in similar situations. Central to this process is collection of local evidence on what is happening in order to identify preferred options for the future and sharing this information with those who will be affected.

A recent report from the Union of Concerned Scientists focuses on the eastern seaboard of the USA and the flood threat faced by dozens of cities, from Washington DC to Miami.[13] It is a wake-up call of the highest order given that the timescale needed to implement appropriate adaption to rising sea levels can take decades. More frequent tidal flooding is already occurring and causing increasing disruption. The report calculates that many on the towns of the east coast will see a tripling of floods by 2030 and ten times as many floods by 2045. This has huge implications for all aspects of urban infrastructure, from homes, transport and communications to where people live, work and go about their daily lives. The threat to economic output is considerable, the challenge to local and state government enormous. Over the next 15 to 30 years, the report highlights, the impact of tidal flooding on the east coast cities of America will be widespread, frequent and disruptive. Problems such as these are increasingly occurring in many coastal areas of the world, including our own.

All coastal areas will need to adapt to rising sea levels in some way. In the broadest terms three types of adaptation are possible, retreating before the sea and letting some low lying areas revert to salt marsh, defending against the waves with higher sea walls and breakwaters or moving out into the coastal zone with stilted or even floating buildings (see report above). Such decisions will be influenced by economic costs and practical priorities, as well as by the nature of coastal settlements, whether tourist resorts, busy seaports or wild territory. Many of the required projects will be extremely expensive to build and take decades to complete. If you live near the coast you should check out the current and future situation in order to consider longer term options.

## Seeing adaptation solutions

Stephen Sheppard argues that we often don't recognise adaptation activity in the community because we are not tuned in to what it actually looks like.[14] He uses a wide selection of photographs and examples to show what we might be missing. Examples are many and various. Piles of sandbags in a garden or a council yard show local people know they must now be prepared for flooding. In the Netherlands you can see neighbourhoods that can float as water levels change. Covered walkways and tree sheltered areas provide spaces to shelter from the sun. Painting roofs white helps reflect heat away. New sea walls and river defences are increasingly seen and beaches restored after storm surges. Basins may be excavated to trap and hold rainwater before letting it soak away. Drought tolerant gardens and permeable driveways are becoming more common. The need to build greater local self-reliance may be demonstrated by backyard vegetable plots, allotments, farm shops and farmers' markets. Harvesting water from roofs will become more common. These are all examples of how we can begin to recognise and be inspired by adaptation to climate change.

Whilst we all need to understand the ways in which we personally need to adapt to this, it is equally a matter for every household, workplace and community, as well as for companies, industries, local, regional and national government. It is useful, therefore, to consider practical examples of adaptation in their wider context. The Environment Agency has an attractive set of six cutaway diagrams entitled 'Future Worlds 2030' which illustrate what adaptation will begin to look like in various local contexts.[15] Some of the main elements are summarised below. They each illustrate features designed to reduce the negative effects of climate change and to exploit opportunities for positive change.

## Domestic house

Window design involves double-glazed windows which provide both insulation and natural ventilation, shutters provide shade and screens are used to keep disease carrying insects out. Outside the driveway is made of permeable material so water can easily drain away as part of a sustainable drainage system. The garden contains drought resistant plants, trees to provide shade and a pond for additional drainage. In the house power points are high enough to avoid flood damage, grey water (from showers etc) and rainwater are captured and reused, whilst floors are raised to help guard against flooding.

## Cityscape

Road surfaces are made from materials better able to cope with higher temperatures and heavy rain. Better drainage systems can cope with intense and heavy rainfall. Building may be raised to guard against flooding and to ensure comfort for users in higher temperatures. Natural ventilation and insulation will be important here. Roofs could be 'green' to reduce water run-off, aid biodiversity and lessen the urban heat island effect, white to reflect heat or with solar panels.

## Coastal

A new harbour wall protects the port against rising sea level and new tide gates keep extreme tidal surges at bay. Cranes are designed to work in higher temperatures. Commercial fisheries and aquaculture have shifted emphasis in the face of rising sea temperatures and changing fish stocks. Offshore wind farms play a vital role in energy production linked to onshore substations and a decentralised grid. Some coastal areas have been allowed to return to salt marsh or mudflats easing pressure on local flood defences. Well-protected tourism is on the increase.

## Major infrastructure

Stronger railway track prevents buckling in high temperatures and embankments are strengthened to cope with wetter winters and drier summers. River bridges are higher to match a larger tidal range with reinforced foundations to cope with floods. Motorway surfaces have been adapted to cope with higher temperatures and heavy rain. Central reservations have emergency gates allowing traffic to turn round if the road ahead is impassable. Tougher telecom cabling is designed to resist higher temperatures, groundwater flooding and subsidence. Pylons are designed to withstand extreme weather events and to avoid excess wire expansion when temperatures are high. Reservoirs are strengthened to prevent dam-burst after extreme rainfall and covered in summer to minimise water loss through evaporation.

## Future farm

Longer growing seasons and less frost has resulted in crop diversification, such as grapes and olives. There are changes in crop varieties, as well as planting and harvesting to match hotter and drier summers. Changes in land management prevent soil erosion. Increased rainfall is managed through tree planting and sustainable drainage via porous surfaces and ponds. Trees provide shade for animals (reducing heat stress) and a source of renewable fuel. A combined heat and power unit, which reduces carbon emissions and increases energy security, uses local wood to heat crop storage facilities. Awareness of sustainable farming is raised through the farm shop and cafe which is also a response to increased domestic tourism.

## Countryside

More information is made available on the risks of wildfire, with improvement to emergency access and water storage for fire-fighting. Reinforced footpaths are provided to reduce tourist erosion arising from hotter, drier summers. Recreating floodplains where rivers were previously straightened helps hold water during flooding and enriches wildlife. Species are given the best possible opportunities to adapt to warming climate. Creation and conservation of a wide range of habitats now supports a wide variety of species. Retained and increased woodland, scrub and peat bog help to slow water flow in heavy rain.

These examples of adaptation provide a series of snapshots of necessary change. If we are to stay safe and comfortable the responsibility for planning and initiating such changes arises at every level of society. Proactive citizens need to start finding out more about the likely weather changes in their region and the immediate adaptation that needs to be made or planned for in the near future. What is my responsibility here to family, friends and neighbours in my vicinity? What conversations need to be had with others and how is this best approached? What is happening in my street, neighbourhood, community or parish? Where can I get support, where can I give support? There is often more going on at local and regional levels than at first meets the eye. In many situations it is still a question of joining up the dots to see what sort of picture they make, whether in relation to adaptation to climate change or limitation (see next chapter). Become an expert, or at least more informed, about what is happening in the county, regionally and nationally. Which organisations, networks and political parties are the most forward looking in these matters? Which would you be prepared to support and which do you feel can most support you.

# 9. Limiting climate change

*A stitch in time saves nine*

- Old proverb[1]

Adaptation and mitigation are the terms used for the two sides of the coin which make up climate change action. To mitigate something is to limit its impact and in the context of this book I use these two terms to mean the same thing. Whilst the last chapter looked at the sorts of changes society will have to deal with in the face of climate change this chapter focuses on what is being done, and what needs to be done, in order to help stem creation of the greenhouse gases which cause global warming in the first place. The United Nations Environment Programme (UNEP) elaborates as follows.

> Climate change mitigation refers to efforts to reduce or prevent emission of greenhouse gases. Mitigation can mean using new technologies and renewable energies, making older equipment more efficient, or changing management practices or consumer behaviour. It can be as complex as a new city, or as simple as improvements to a cooking stove design. Efforts underway around the world range from hi-tech subway systems to bicycling paths and walkways. Protecting natural carbon sinks like forests and oceans, or creating new sinks through silviculture or green agriculture are also elements of mitigation. UNEP takes a multifaceted approach towards climate change mitigation in its efforts to help countries move towards a low-carbon society.[2]

Mitigation requires that we revisit the main greenhouse gases and the ways in which they are created in order to clarify the action required to phase them out as quickly as possible. The

136

longer this process takes the more difficult countering climate change will be. The sooner this is comprehensively done the lower the impacts may be. This does not mean we can stop global warming as this is not possible due to the 200 years of carbon emissions that have already occurred. What we can do is work to limit and stop current emissions as soon as we possibly can.

The world's average global temperature has warmed by 1.0C since pre-industrial times and it is generally agreed we need to keep the increase to no more than 2C by 2050. Any more than this will present us with serious problems. In the UK we need to reduce emissions by between 3 percent and 1 percent per annum.[3] Given the seriousness of this task it will require concerted action at personal, community and national levels. The wider and deeper context for this is the struggle between two major cultural narratives, the old unsustainable high-carbon story and its successor, the new sustainable low-carbon story. Stories such as these underpin our views of economics, politics, environment, technology and indeed the meaning of life. They are at the heart of any discussion about climate change whether overtly, or more commonly, staying unspoken in the background. Action to limit the effects of climate change needs to take place in the family, the community, nationally and internationally.

## Housing

House and home is a good place to start, not least because so many older houses are draughty and uncomfortable, with much of the heat leaking out through roofs, walls, windows, doors and gaps. Randall and Brown show just how different a typical UK house today is compared with what a low-carbon house might look like in 2050, or sooner one hopes. They also provide detailed advice on how to put into effect mitigation in the home.

## CASE STUDY - Low carbon housing

### Typical UK house now

26,000 kWh energy in/6 tonnes $CO_2$ out

    X draughty doors and windows
    X solid brick walls
    X unfilled cavity walls
    X poor insulation
    X ancient boiler
    X single glazing
    X lights left on
    X Inefficient appliances
    X uninformed owner or tenant

### Low carbon housing in 2050

5,000 kWh energy in/1 tonne $CO_2$ out

    ✓ everything draught-stripped
    ✓ super-thick insulation
    ✓ triple glazing
    ✓ heating from a renewable source
    ✓ heat recovery ventilation
    ✓ solar panels
    ✓ LED lights
    ✓ smart meters
    ✓ efficient appliances
    ✓ energy-conscious owner or tenant

Source: Randall and Brown [3]

Whilst building regulations have been improving in the UK, there is still much that needs to be done to ensure this quality of building. To reduce the carbon emissions of a house two things need to be done: reducing the amount of energy required in its construction, i.e. the materials it is made up of, and ensuring the energy it then runs on comes from renewable sources. Different political parties may wish to support owners and tenants in this work through grants and green deals or to leave it to the free market forces. It is worth considering therefore which parties are most up-front in their commitment to effective adaptation and mitigation.

## Food

How does the food we eat relate to climate mitigation? To answer that question one needs to know more about how one's food is grown and where it comes from. Contemporary large-scale farming, whether in the UK or elsewhere, has a high carbon footprint. The first enquiry has to be about where food has come from and how far it has travelled. When I was a child in the 1950s more of the food I ate, bread, meat, fruit and vegetables, came from the UK than it does today. It was generally not processed, required minimal packaging, with refrigerators and freezers in the home not yet common. The carbon footprint of people's diets then was much smaller than it is now. Today food is shipped from all over the world by sea, air and road, guaranteeing high 'food miles' and therefore a high carbon footprint. The length of such journeys together with the manufacture and disposal of wasteful over-packaging adds to the footprint. Farming itself became increasingly industrialised after World War 2 and has long been dependent on a wide range of herbicides, pesticides, feedstuffs and other practices derived from by-products of coal and oil. So producing food and eating what we like are both high-carbon activities. If this had not been clear before it is because this lack of insight is embedded in the old high-carbon story.

The new story about food is not only about the need to eat more healthily and avoid obesity it is also about reducing the carbon footprint of our meals and snacks. One of the reasons why people have become more interested in where their food comes from relates to food miles. There are now many farm shops and food suppliers across the UK who source their produce as locally as they can. They can explain exactly where and how your food was grown and it also keeps money within the local community rather than exporting it to distant food companies. The three carbon threads that need to be challenged and diminished here are: the distance food travels, the packaging that it comes in and the ways in which it has been grown. This is why there has been a resurgence of interest in more locally sourced food, in easily disposed of low-carbon packaging, grown organically or using natural methods.[4]

A good example of community action and education in this sphere is Transition Chepstow's local food challenge.

## CASE STUDY - Chepstow Local Food Challenge

The challenge we set ourselves was 'for a month, to eat as far as possible, food grown or produced within a 30 mile radius of Chepstow'. We chose September because a good range of local fruit and vegetables is available then.

Our aims were:

- to see if we could reduce our carbon footprint by eating locally
- to see what it would be like if we had to be reliant on local food
- to celebrate the food that is available locally.
- We put together a Local Food Directory and were surprised at how much was available within our radius. The Town Council supported the challenge by putting on extra Farmers Markets in the town. Nearly everyone said they found taking part in the food challenge a positive experience. Reasons included:
- explored new local foods.... enjoyed learning about others' experiences
- having to think differently about what to buy

- a focus on what was and wasn't available locally

- joining with others to support local producers and the economy

We asked participants what they were able to buy from local sources, and the answers were revealing: vegetables 100 percent; meat/fish 87 percent; fruit 80 percent; dairy 60 percent; drinks 47 percent; cereals 0 percent

Most people said that there would be lasting effects from the food challenge:

- 93 per cent will eat more local food

- 93 per cent will shop in places that sell local food

- 85 per cent are more interested in where food comes from

- 69 per cent will grow more food

We hope the Food Challenge will not be a one-off event but part of continuing activity to develop Chepstow as a town with a buoyant local food economy. In particular, we would like to see weekly markets thriving, more shops stocking local food and drink, more pubs and restaurants in the town using local produce, and a wider range of local produce available.

Source: Transition Chepstow [5]

Further advice on mitigating the carbon impact of food in one's life can be found in *The Carbon Conversations Handbook*.[6]

## Transport

Today we take it for granted that we can travel where we like, when we like, as often as we like, but this has not always been the norm. It is only in the last fifty years that travel and transport have changed to what we take as normal today. The distances we are prepared to travel have become longer as has the time spent on this. And this is another of our norms that comes directly out of the old high-carbon narrative. The travel and transportation that we take so for granted has brought enormous benefits but, due to its high carbon footprint, is now acknowledged as a significant contributor to climate change.

Car ownership in particular has become inextricably bound up with our own sense of self-image and freedom. When American industrialist Henry Ford proclaimed, 'I will build a car for the great multitude,' he could never have realised how globally ubiquitous the car would become nor how deeply it would influence human culture. Neither could he and others have possibly understood then the wider climate impact of this on future generations. The car has become so much part of people's psyches that it is now bound up with our deepest sense of status, belonging and security. Manufacturers know exactly how to play on this carefully fostered relationship as so many car adverts demonstrate.

In broad terms there is only a limited number of mitigation options available. The main ones are: driving more efficiently, driving shorter distances, using technology to get better fuel consumption, using fuels that have no carbon footprint, using other forms of transport. More efficient driving requires less use of brakes and fast acceleration, settling for a lower speed overall and turning off the engine when idling. This can give lower petrol consumption and cut fuel costs. It is, however, the thin edge of what needs to be a much bigger wedge. This is why hybrid and electric cars are beginning to gain a significant foothold on the market. As the range of electric cars increases and availability of charging points becomes more common so will this form of transport. Similarly hybrid cars are becoming more popular, with their combination of petrol engine and electric battery. At low speeds the battery drives the car, when the petrol motor kicks in it charges up the battery, so no external source is needed to do this. When stationary the engine cuts out but automatically comes on when the accelerator is touched. The engine is in the lowest emission band. However, all of this needs careful checking in the face of the misleading figures given out by various car manufacturers. The use of biofuels is also often seen as a solution to vehicle emissions. However, this brings its own problems because the large-scale growing of crops for biofuel means less farmland is available for the growing of much needed food crops globally. Something like a quarter of all the maize and grain crops grown in the US is now used to create biofuel as against being used to feed people. One useful site for advice on low-carbon driving is Next Green Car.[7]

However, cars are only one mode of transport so mitigating their impact can also be done by using public forms of transport more often - tram, bus, coach and rail. These forms of transport carry more people per mile and therefore have a much lower carbon footprint than cars. In the days before we nearly all had cars, these forms of transport were much more commonly used and taken as the norm. Electric trams, trains and cars will still have a carbon footprint unless their power comes from an energy company sourced entirely by renewable energy, such as Good Energy or Ecotricity. These forms of public transport are a vital part of the low-carbon way forward. The information sheet below is a reminder of the vital role of city planning in setting out an overall policy in these matters, giving direction and encouragement from above and demonstrating the vital importance of joined-up thinking.

## CASE STUDY - Newcastle: Go Zero

Go Zero is Newcastle City Council's campaign to help reduce the city's carbon footprint by encouraging our residents to travel by more sustainable modes.

Whilst we have done a lot to promote walking and cycling throughout the city, there are a number of other ways to travel more sustainably. Did you know that we have a city-wide car club, one of the largest electric vehicle charge-point networks in Europe and a park and ride facility that offers free parking and frequent rapid connections to the city centre? We have also created the Go Zero app to help you travel more sustainably.

### Car Club

Newcastle City Council is working with Co-wheels Car Club to offer a convenient greener and cheaper alternative to owning your own car. Why not join today and start saving money, reducing your carbon footprint and removing the hassle of car ownership?

### Electric Vehicles

The North East is leading the way in the development of electric car use, and leading the charge when it comes to installing electric vehicle charging points.

With over 80 charge points throughout the city we recognise the growing demand for greener travel and we are striving to provide a widespread network across the city to encourage the use of electric vehicles.

*Park and Ride*

Do you regularly travel between Great Park, Gosforth and Newcastle City Centre? Sick of getting stuck in traffic on your way to and from work? Spending a fortune on city centre parking? Then why not take the hassle out of your journey with our new park and ride services? Park for free at our Newcastle Great Park and Ride facility and then avoid the traffic by jumping on board our rapid X40 service. It'll save you both time and money!

Join the **Go Zero** sustainable transport campaign and find out how you could save money and reduce your carbon footprint today.

Source: Newcastle City Council [8]

## Consuming

Some two-hundred years ago the poet William Wordsworth, looking at the bustling city of London from Westminster Bridge, observed 'The world is too much with us; late and soon/getting and spending, we lay waste our powers'. Of the many things that humans could commit themselves to - a more just and peaceful world, collaboration and cooperation, protection and nourishment of the natural world - how come so many have settled for 'getting and spending'? There are many other things that humans value highly, whether dignity and wisdom, empathy and compassion or solidarity and hard graft. True, material things involve shelter, food, clothes and being able to earn a living, they are the first prerequisites, the basics of human comfort and there are many other needs than this. But why is there such a compulsion for acquiring 'things' beyond our actual needs? Conspicuous consumption does, of course, have a long history, it showed that rulers, politicians, leaders or the top one per cent had arrived, or were always there, surrounded by the trappings of power. They could also afford to throw wealth away without batting an eyelid.

So historically we have many such examples, although relatively speaking confined to the few. The wealth generated by the Industrial Revolution raised people's material expectations of what was meant by the 'good life'. As we saw in chapter 5 the twentieth century saw a rapid rise in the availability and marketing of consumer goods - cars, TVs, washing machines, clothes, luxuries - to a wider and wider audience and the constant advertising of even more goods people did not necessarily need but were persuaded that they did. This notion of having more became associated both with self-importance and the notion that this was what progress was really all about. In this notion of success and happiness the limits to growth have been and are constantly exceeded (chapter 3). Most manufacturing and use of resources to make more things has its own in-built carbon footprint. When we throw away a drinks can after a few seconds' satisfaction we add to our own carbon footprint because of the carbon embodied in that object. A visit to the council tip graphically illustrates the monumental volume of waste that we create and want to put out of sight, generally in someone else's country or ecological habitat. Thus the low-carbon mantra: rethink, refuse, reduce, reuse, recycle.

It is the free-market form of economics which particularly stresses the need for constantly growing economies, constant exploitation of resources and people to feed our inflated appetites. Our overconsumption of the planet's resources is unsustainable and this needs challenging in the light of climate change. Indeed the five-fold mantra cited above can be used to illuminate and expand on the notion of limitation. Firstly, we need to *rethink* all aspects of our daily lives in the light of climate change and the need to create a more sustainable future. It is to be hoped this book is helping in such rethinking or perhaps confirming previous trains of thought. Given the interrelated big ideas being explored here it may also sometimes feel worrying or disorientating. At first, rethinking something through can often feel like this. But the most important thing is being open to new ideas and perspectives. Mull things over, stay open-minded, think of the ways in which such changes may enhance the safety of your family and the future of your community.

Next one needs to focus on what one needs to *refuse*, what one wants to say 'no' to. This is not necessarily a negative position but a positive one, especially if it has come out of a period of rethinking. Being clear about what one wants to say 'no' to also helps one identify what one wants to say 'yes' to. Going back to chapter 3 it might be that you feel you want to say 'no' to unsustainable practices and 'yes' to those which enhance sustainability. It might just feel like a gut instinct at this stage. You then need to read further and check what the key features of unsustainability/sustainability look like in a particular context or in relation to a particular issue such as housing, food or transport. Once a 'no' seems clear it is often then easier to identify the alternative 'yes'.

These first two stages clarify and clear quite a lot of ground before one gets to *reduce*. Reducing in this context might be choosing to eat food grown more locally, to make fewer car journeys, to reduce your personal carbon footprint (see chapter 10). Amongst other things reduction can help make things simpler and clearer. It might be about taking things to the recycling centre, only buying things that you really need or spending more time in the natural environment. In the end it is about limiting the things you do and buy that contribute to global warming and thus playing your small but vitally important part in mitigating climate change. It is interesting that it is the last two elements of the mantra which are often best known. One can *reuse* all sorts of items, whether old timber and glass jars or mended clothes and repaired equipment. Indeed mending and reusing was taken as the norm by previous generations. You didn't throw a pair of shoes away, you took them to the shoe shop to be mended. You didn't throw away your old TV or radio, you took it to the shop to be repaired. Not least it was cheaper than having to buy new items. Now we throw away whole items because we cannot get the small part repaired which is all that was needed.

*Recycling* by the local council has been around for a long time. Some object because they cannot see the point or because they produce large volumes of waste themselves. With kerbside collection of items or materials that need to be taken to the recycling centre, things can be used again in a similar or different form that prolong their useful life. They do not add to vast landfill sites nor require materials to be used in making new products with their own carbon footprint. The last of the five steps is the one best known, if only grudgingly accepted by some. What would it look like if all children at home and in school were brought up with all these steps as being perfectly everyday and normal?

Annie Leonard, in *The Story of Stuff*, sets out a clear and comprehensive account of how we misuse natural resources, from extraction and production to distribution, consumption and disposal. Her advice in the context of US over-consumption is summarised here.

## *Opposing advertising*

1. Decommercialise our culture. Reclaim our mental and physical landscape from commercial advertisers. Ban billboards and other intrusive advertising. Prohibit commercial advertising to children and in public places. Get commercial advertising out of textbooks, classrooms and all educational facilities. The Campaign for a Commercial-Free Childhood conducts research and advocates for protective policies; to get involved visit www.commercialexploitation.org
2. Ensure public investment in commons like libraries, athletic facilities, and parks so that residents can meet their needs and enjoy leisure time without buying Stuff. Attend city council meetings to voice your opinion about budget priorities, or better yet, run for office yourself!

3. Adopt a progressive tax on resource consumption, allowing free use for basic needs while taxing higher-quality use. For example, water to drink is free; water to wash your SUV or water your desert lawn is really expensive. A vibrant and often heated discussion is happening on the international level as to what constitutes basic needs.

Source: Leonard [9]

## Reforestation

Whether directly or indirectly from goods bought we need to be much less responsible for deforestation. Trees are not just a source of timber but also an important habitat for wildlife and in particular, they absorb and store large amounts of $CO_2$ from the atmosphere. Forests are also unique ecosystems containing thousands of animal and plant species. All plants absorb $CO_2$ but trees have been likened to the lungs of the planet given the huge scale on which they do this. Forests are an example of what is called a 'carbon sink' because they are able to trap large amounts of carbon dioxide and in so doing they help mitigate climate change. Deforestation, an almost worldwide phenomenon, is responsible for about 20 per cent of greenhouse gas emissions as the result of both legal and illegal logging. This is why sustainable forestry is so important, the planting of new trees to equal or exceed the number that have been cut down and allowing for the time they take to grow to maturity.

Forests are vitally important habitats and a crucial part of the complex jigsaw which is our ecosystem. They are also a huge resource containing many known, and as yet unknown, plant species vital to medicine and medical knowledge. 1 in 4 ingredients in our medicine come from rainforest plants. Reforestation is thus a vital task for logging companies, government initiatives, numerous local action groups and families in order to capture and absorb $CO_2$. Sustainable forestry is good for the planet and all those who inhabit it, human and non-human. Planting a tree or a small wood really is looking after future generations and beginning to mitigate one's own carbon footprint, something explored further in the next chapter. It is also important to recall that forests support the livelihoods of around one in six people on the planet.[10]

## Seeing mitigation solutions

As mentioned in the previous chapter we often don't recognise adaptation and mitigation in the community because we are not always aware of what we're looking at. It's not that we don't actually see examples of climate change mitigation in our travels. We do, but may not actually recognise them as such. Examples are many and various. If one lives near the coast or is visiting such an area one may see offshore wind farms in the distance supplying low-carbon renewable energy. Inland one may glimpse solar farms where hundreds of panels at low level are angled to catch the sun's rays. Not far from where I live there is a single wind generator funded by the local community which use most of its energy and similar individual turbines are springing up elsewhere. Sometimes on the nearby railway I see long goods trains with covered wagons passing which move such goods off the roads, reducing traffic and carbon emissions.

When seeing friends in a city I find myself admiring their tram system with its links to railway terminals and local suburbs. I get a lift when I think of the contribution this makes to reducing dangerous street pollution. I also like seeing electric vehicles (EVs) and hybrids and noting where charging points are located. On rooftops I sometimes see solar thermal water heating, or more often photovoltaic solar panels on town houses, country barns and industrial estates. If I'm on foot I may pass a house where improved energy efficiency work is going on, with exterior walls being insulated and triple glazing put in the windows. Wood burning stoves can replace high-carbon forms of indoor heating such as coal and oil. A large new shed tucked behind a local hotel turned out to shelter a new woodchip boiler, sourced from local forestry and heating the whole building. Busy gardens and local allotments can produce a significant proportion of residents' food with a lower carbon footprint. Smart meters in the home give instant feedback on energy consumption.

Once we have learnt to recognize these features as examples of climate change mitigation we then begin to see many more in our neighbourhood, on journeys and in other countries. We need to share and explain what we are seeing with others, whether children, students, friends or family. What we are seeing is the new low-carbon story at work around us. It is really important to recognise what it is we are seeing - the foundations of a more clean, safe and sustainable society. The task is to help this to grow. As witness to this a recent article announced 'Renewable energy outstrips coal for the first time in UK electricity mix'.

> Renewable energy has for the first time surpassed coal in supplying the UK's electricity for a whole quarter, according to government statistics... The revelation of the surge in wind, solar and bioenergy to a record 25% comes in a week when the government has been heavily criticised by business leaders and Al Gore for cutting support for clean energy.
>
> The high performance of renewable electricity between April and June, the latest period data is available for, was due to both more wind and sun, more turbines and solar panels having been installed, compared to the same period the year before, when renewable contributed 16.4% of electricity.
>
> Gas-fired power stations provided the most electricity - 30% - with renewable second. Nuclear power was third with 21.5% and coal - the most polluting fuel, fell back to fourth, with 20.5%. Aging coal and nuclear plants have been closing in recent years, while renewable energy has been rapidly rolling out.[11]

Because the need for limitation and adaptation have been around for several decades it is not surprising that examples are increasingly visible in the community and across the country. Neither is it surprising to find evidence that the low-carbon shift is beginning to appear in all sorts of figures and statistics. Examples of both adaptation and mitigation are increasingly visible and measurable in our daily lives. If we do not know what they look like we will fail to see them and possibly dismiss their existence. Once we can connect what we know with what we can see on a daily basis interest grows and encourages further involvement and action.

We have now tracked climate change from its causes and impacts to a wide range of required solutions, named broadly adaptation and mitigation. Behind these two terms lies a world of difference, the difference between walking unthinkingly into the future and walking well prepared into it. We cannot afford to walk backwards into the future because being prepared in a variety of different ways is always safer, both for ourselves and those for whom we have responsibility. Our parents and grandparents may have had tough decisions to make in their own time as we do in ours, but ours are of a different order, a sustainable low-carbon future.

# Part Four

## A journey of hope

# 10. Telling family stories

*Home is where one starts from*

- Poet T.S. Eliot[1]

At this point it is important to recap where we have got to in the story about changing climate. Part 1 set out the broad causes, consequences and impacts of climate change and how this arose from use of fossil fuels over the last two hundred years in order to meet the needs of society. It also raised the crucial question of what sort of society we want to help create, both for ourselves and younger generations. High-carbon 'business as usual' will lead to increasingly difficult climate change and a socially and environmentally unsustainable future. Transitioning to a clean, low-carbon economy offers the possibility of a safer and more sustainable future but still with a changing climate. Part 2 explored some of the emotional difficulties arising in this context and set out the main features of the old high-carbon story that now needs to put aside and its successor, the new low-carbon story, which we need to learn and share. Part 3 explored the responsibility we have to learn more about positive ways of adapting to climate change and limiting some of its impacts.

Part 4 concludes by looking at examples of good climate change practice in relation to home, school and community. Taken together this is where such practice is already beginning to occur and which now needs to become the new norm. These activities at a local grassroots level are about gathering resources for a journey of hope. It's not as if we were given the opportunity to tick a low-carbon or a high-carbon box when we arrived on this planet. We are born into circumstances not of our choosing and have to do the best we can with the cards we've been dealt. It would seem we have all now drawn one which says 'Avoid danger - proceed to low- carbon option now'.

## The new Home Front

A number of people have looked at the global situation we find ourselves in and seen parallels with the Second World War and possible lessons that could be drawn on from that period. In the 1930s many politicians ignored the threat of war that was brewing and did nothing at the time to deter aggression or make preparations to defend the UK. Yet during the war people made great sacrifices to defeat Nazism and build a fairer society. All sorts of organisations mobilised themselves for change, from voluntary groups and churches to schools, universities and public services. Whilst it was not clear at the time whether this mobilisation would be effective or not it proved itself to great effect - energy consumption dropped, food consumption fell, kitchen waste was saved, scrap metal was recycled. In the face of serious adversity both government and population radically changed their mindset. What could the public do today to tackle climate change if we were on the equivalent of such a 'war footing'? Every home and household counted then and every home and household counts now.[2]

Sharon Astyk comments:

> We may use war as an analogy, but we should remember it is only that; this is not about fighting but about regeneration...We know that once Americans and the British were joined in a great endeavour. It was difficult, tragic and harrowing - but it also made the people who endured it great and gave us a future we could not have had under fascism. It was terribly hard because it demanded that ordinary people became heroes to save themselves and future generations. And if we are to go forward from where we are, we must believe that we are their honourable descendants who, like our parents and grandparents and great-grandparents, have the courage and love for the future to make heroic sacrifices and unite quite literally to save the world.[3]

One might argue that it worked then because government eventually took the lead and had the vision to conceive the changes that were necessary in the economy and the community to help win the war. Interestingly, a recent report pointed out that whatever cuts governments pledge to make in carbon emissions internationally, it will not be sufficient unless firm action is also taken at a local level.[4] In the face of current governmental cuts to support for renewables it's worth remembering MP Tim Yeo's comment, when chair of the cross-party energy and climate change committee, that 'Cutting spending on low carbon technologies now would be like cutting the budget for Spitfires in 1939'.[5]

## Story time

Chapter 5 looked at different sorts of stories and their importance in making sense of our lives. In particular it focused on the nature of cultural narratives which gradually build up over historical time to give an account of what that culture or society believes its purpose to be. At the other end of the scale we have short and carefully tailored stories we tell to children and young people in order to help them in their understanding as they are growing up. These may literally be family stories, i.e. stories about family members past and present which are memorable, amusing or contain a particular lesson it might be useful to learn. Then there are the stories children tell each other or read about that become woven, directly or indirectly, into their lives. In particular there are elements of the cultural narrative that children pick up about history, other people and notions of right and wrong. I was taught the old high-carbon story as a boy by my parents, everyone I knew, school and life generally. Of course, I didn't know then it was a misleading and dangerous story or even that it was a story. Neither did those around me because, as is always the case with cultural narratives, those deep beliefs were not even seen as story but the accepted taken-for-granted way of understanding and making sense of the world. I had to wait till much later in life to become aware of that. So what we say in passing, both indirectly and directly to children really matters. They need to begin to learn, if they have not already done so, key elements of the low-carbon story.

Sharon Astyk reflects on the role that parents have today.

> There is no need for children to know all the bad news. Make adaptation fun - talk about how nice the new way of doing things is, or discuss living like people did long ago. Older children need more truth than younger ones, but don't rush it - or overprotect them...

> We must begin to prepare, both at the personal level in our own homes and communities and by advocating for larger solutions. But all of us have limited time and energy; so being able to narrow our focus and decide what we must do is as important as knowing that we must prepare...

> It seems to me that the only way to give the next generation a decent shot at life is for those of us who care most about them to take things into our own hands and prepare for the changes ahead.[6]

I used to say to my students, some of whom were going to be primary teachers, there were two things children learnt at home - that when you press a switch there will always be electricity and when you turn on a tap there will always be water. The point I was making was that, unless told otherwise, this is as far as the story of electricity and water may go, a very incomplete picture of two vital resources. The story of water starts with the water cycle and how rain falling from the clouds onto hills and into valleys, is collected in reservoirs and then fed by pipeline to towns and cities. After its use in homes and factories it is treated at the sewage works and goes back on its way to the sea, where evaporation takes moisture back into the clouds. To really understand water one needs to understand all the details of this cycle. Fresh water is not inexhaustible, it shouldn't be wasted - we also have a water footprint. Similarly, where does our electricity come from? What sort of power station creates it and how does it work? Does it come from fossil fuels or renewable sources of energy? What different impacts do these have on people and the environment? These things should be taught in school when children are young but also needs to be backed-up at home. Conversely, the school story of how these things work needs to be supported by what is learnt at home.

The explanations that we give children need to be age appropriate and often will be part of the household instructions we want children to remember - Can I hear a tap running? Have you switched the lights off? Did you put it in the recycling box? There can also be simple explanations for younger children about changing climate. For example:

> 'Fossil fuels (coal, oil and gas) were once seen as a great idea because they helped build our busy world. But then it was found that using them to make electricity or fuel for transport also warmed up our atmosphere! This warming began to melt the ice where polar bears live and to make the weather more changeable, so what had looked like a good idea now looked not so good. Today other sources of energy are being used (sun, wind and water) which can't get used up because they are renewable and they don't warm up our atmosphere. So that's really great for us and the animals too.'

Or perhaps on a wider scale when older:

> 'Once upon a time there was a blue-green planet, a good place to live, out on the edge of a spiral galaxy that looked like this. The people who lived there had grown pretty clever and so they spent their time inventing as many things as they could possibly think of.

Many of these things were very useful, but it also turned out that some of the things they invented weren't actually good at all for the planet or the people. The better-off people on the planet were having a mad party and they said 'Why should we stop doing this? This is what life is all about! Stop being a spoil-sport!'

However, there were other more thoughtful and wiser people who said, 'But actually this big party is using up the planet's resources too quickly. And the mess we're making is now changing this place which is our home. We haven't got anywhere else to go so we better start clearing up our act before things get worse.' And so they did. What do you think were some of the things that they changed?'

Children are naturally inquisitive and one should always support this meaning-making process by answering their questions in as helpful a way as possible but also posing questions to them at appropriate moments: Where do you think our energy comes from? What impact does it have on our environment? Can we use renewable energy here? How energy efficient is our house? How energy efficient can we become? Are there any local schemes to help make older houses more energy efficient? Where is the nearest place to see examples of low-carbon buildings? Where can we see solar panels/a wind farm? The answers to questions such as these may require a bit of homework first. There will certainly be some examples of low-carbon activity not too far away. Or it may not be much of an issue at all. My grandchildren live in Cornwall and take it for granted that they are surrounded by wind turbines and solar panels. That's just how it is and it doesn't really need commenting on - it's normal. They were also fortunate to be brought up in a way that gave them a love of the outdoors, both locally and elsewhere - exploring the countryside, learning to read maps, camping out, climbing mountains, kayaking on lakes, rivers and around the coast. As they grew older I watched them develop a sense of adventure, a respect for wild places and knowing how to stay safe in different environments. The natural world for them is a place of adventure, excitement, peace and quiet, awe and wonder. Not everyone can necessarily do this for their children but enjoying the outdoors, playing in nature, finding interesting things to see and do, is possible in all sorts of ways. From this can come a respectful attitude to nature and an understanding that the biosphere requires our intelligent protection and care.

## Carbon footprints

Previous chapters set out in some detail the sort of work that is being done in relation to adaptation and limitation and the reasons for this. One widely used way of identifying the amount of carbon being emitted by an activity, person, business or even a country, is by measuring their 'carbon footprint'. Mike Berners-Lee and Duncan Clark explain this as follows.

> When talking about climate change, *footprint* is a metaphor for the total impact that something has. And *carbon* is shorthand for all the different greenhouse gases that contribute to global warming. The term *carbon footprint*, therefore, is a shorthand to describe the best estimate that we can get of the full climate impact of something. That something could be anything - an activity, an item, a lifestyle, a company, a country or even the whole world.[7]

Most importantly they remind us that things can often get left out when calculating a carbon footprint. For example, one might work out the footprint of one's home in relation to energy consumed but forget to include daily travel and purchase of goods. Another important, but often unacknowledged distinction, is that between 'direct' and 'indirect' carbon emissions. The true carbon footprint of a new TV, for example, is not only the direct energy it uses (and wastes if left on stand-by) but also the indirect footprint of its component parts - the extraction and processing of the materials which its components are made of.

It's also possible to calculate the footprint of different countries, whilst noting that poorer countries have a much lower carbon footprint than the rich world and are thus much less responsible for climate change. The Carbon Footprint Calculator cites:

- The average footprint for people in the United Kingdom is 9.80 tonnes per annum
- The average for the industrial nations is about 11 tonnes
- The average worldwide carbon footprint is about 4 tonnes
- The worldwide target to combat climate change is 2 tonnes per person[8]

The worldwide target of only two tonnes of carbon emissions per person is because it's been calculated that anything higher than this is likely to increase global warming by more than 2C which could lead to irreversible change. Internationally governments also argue about which countries are most responsible for climate change. This is a crucial issue because, as mentioned above, richer countries have the largest carbon footprint and poorer countries the smallest. The latter group argue that richer countries, the biggest culprits, should therefore bear the major costs of limitation and adaption. A further recent twist is that rich countries are outsourcing their carbon emissions to rising economies such as China. Carbon emissions arising from the manufacture of cheap clothes and electronic devices in China then contribute to that country's footprint. Those who required these products to be brought into existence and who use them then seem to bear no responsibility for the resulting carbon emissions.

There are many examples of how to calculate the carbon footprint of an item, person, home or family. Mike Berners-Lee is really good on this in his book *How Bad Are Bananas? The carbon footprint of everything*.[9] Another source I've found helpful is the online Carbon Footprint Calculator and I'm taking this as an example to work with.[10] It helps to look through the website first to see what sort of questions you're going to be asked about the family economics. I found, for example, I needed to do a bit of homework on energy bills, travel patterns, food consumption and other family activities. As these figures are filled in the site shows the carbon footprint for each element and finally the total carbon footprint in tonnes. You can then compare this with the national average and also the suggested world target of two tonnes. The first time this is done it often comes as a bit of a surprise. There is, however, a big difference between the starting point and what can be achieved over a period of time as one begins to monitor activities more closely. It helps one become more aware of how different habits, choices and actions contribute to the carbon footprint of the home and it clarifies the decisions and actions that need to be made in order to diminish one's carbon impact. This is the point at which one starts to move in practice from the high to low-carbon story.

This calculator is also useful in that it takes into account the indirect carbon footprint. Thus under food preferences the options to tick are 'vegan/mainly fish/mainly white meat/white and red meat/always red meat'. Red meat has the highest secondary carbon footprint because it has behind it the whole of the livestock industry, the land used for grazing, animal feed, transportation and meat processing. White meat sources take up much less space and transportation. Most fish don't need to be fed by humans. The choices under fashion are, 'I regularly shop to have the latest fashions/I buy new clothes when I need them/I only buy second hand'. The 'latest fashions' option literally uses more resources, the growing and watering of cotton, for example, its harvesting, transport and manufacture into garments, and often sweat-shop labour. Packaging is a vast and often thoughtless industry with a large carbon footprint. Many products are wrapped in excessive and unnecessary packaging which is immediately thrown away, including plastic bags, plastic wrapping, cardboard and cling film, adding to mountains of unnecessary waste.

The carbon footprint is an important guide to the emissions one creates and where, through careful choice, these can be diminished. The overall figure can be compared with national averages or with like-minded friends. My advice would be not to try and change everything at once but start with two or three different aspects. It's important also to get children and young people onside so that it becomes an interesting and creative endeavour together. Talk with friends and colleagues, check monthly how you are getting on, ask local schools what they are doing about their carbon footprint since these low-carbon activities need to become widely recognised as sensible practice.

Importantly, Stephen Sheppard also reminds us:

> While the per capita footprint figures tell a compelling story, they can be somewhat misleading in terms of individual responsibility. We do not directly control all of the national carbon emissions through our day-to-day actions. Individual Canadians, for example, have no say over the high emissions from tar sands, other than possibly by voting down the Federal government.[11]

What to do about the inevitable discrepancies that often appear in one's carbon lifestyle? One thing individuals, homes and companies can do, if they wish, is to choose to offset their carbon footprint. What this means is supporting an activity which is specifically low-carbon in its goals so that it helps make up in part or whole for any discrepancy in one's footprint. This could, for example, be supporting accredited clean energy initiatives, such as a community based wind turbine or wind farm, tree planting in the UK or reforestation projects elsewhere.

Carbon Footprint also offers a quick guide to carbon reduction which is shown below.

## CASE STUDY - Carbon Footprint Reduction

### For individuals

Here's a simple list of things you can do immediately.

- Turn it off when not in use (lights, television, DVD player, Hi Fi, computer)

- Turn down central heating slightly. Just 1 degree will help reduce bill by 8%

- Turn down water heating setting (2 degrees will make significant saving)

- Check the central heating timer setting - remember there is no point heating the house after you have left for work

- Fill dish washer and washing machine with a full load - this will save you water, electricity and washing powder

- Fill the kettle with only as much water as you need

- Do your weekly shopping in a single trip

- Hang out the washing to dry rather than tumble drying it

Following is a list of items that may take an initial investment, but pay for themselves over the course of 1-4 years through savings on your energy bill.

- Fit energy saving light bulbs

- Install thermostatic valves on your radiators

- Insulate your hot water tank, your loft and your walls

- Install cavity wall insulation

- Install 180mm thick loft insulation

- Recycle your grey water

- Replace your old fridge/freezer (if it is over 15 years old), with a new one with energy efficiency rating of 'A'

- Replace your old boiler with a new energy efficient condensing boiler

**Travel less and travel more carbon footprint friendly**

- Car share to work, or for the kids school run

- Use bus or a train rather than your car
- For short journeys either walk or cycle
- Try to reduce the number of flights you take
- See if your employer will allow you to work from home one day a week
- Next time you replace your car - check out low emissions/hybrid/electric
- When staying in a hotel - turn the lights and air-conditioning off when you leave the hotel room, and ask for your room towels to be washed every other day, rather than every day

**As well as your primary carbon footprint, there is also a secondary footprint that you cause through your buying habits**

- Don't buy bottled water if your tap water is safe to drink
- Buy local fruit and vegetables, or even try growing your own
- Buy foods that are in season locally
- Don't buy fruit/vegetables which are out of season, they may have been flown in
- Reduce your consumption of meat
- Try to only buy products made close to home (look out and avoid items that are made in distant lands)
- Buy organic produce
- Don't buy over packaged products
- Recycle as much as possible
- Think carefully about the type of activities you do in your spare time, do any of these cause an increase in carbon emissions? E.g. saunas, health clubs, restaurants, pubs, go-karting etc...

Source: Carbon Footprint [12]

It is important here to clarify the difference between a carbon footprint and an ecological footprint. In particular I have focused on the former because it is carbon emissions (the greenhouse gases) that have led to global warming and climate change. Chapter 3, however, stressed the wider context of human activities and whether they are unsustainable (harmful) or sustainable (beneficial) for both people and the environment. An ecological footprint is thus wider than its carbon footprint counterpart for it includes all the impacts we make on the natural environment, from rivers, lakes and oceans to mining, cropland, grazing land and built-up areas. It is concerned with the sum of what we take from the environment and the waste we put back into the environment. An ecological footprint measures our overall impact on the biosphere which, since it is the planetary life-support system, is important to know.

In terms of household budgets it is always important to know what we have in the bank. Are we running a deficit, sometimes or often overdrawn, do we have a surplus, with money in hand, or do incoming and outgoing generally more or less balance? Our comfort and survival may depend on this. An ecological footprint measures this for the whole planet: is our life-support system overall in balance (sustainable) or deficit (unsustainable)? If an ecosystem is in deficit, that is there are more bads than goods, it is described as being in overshoot. This is how the notion of Earth Overshoot Day came about, mentioned previously. If the global ecological footprint each year matches what the biosphere can process all is well. The books balance as it were on 31 December. If in overshoot the date comes sooner. Earth Overshoot Day in 1970 was December 23, in 2011 it was September 21, in 2015 August 13. This is not as a result of overpopulation but of over consumption, not by all countries but by richer industrialised countries which includes the UK.[13] A sustainable future requires that we live more simply and use less energy, that we have enough to meet our needs but not our greed.

## CASE STUDY - Carbon Conversations

One of the most interesting initiatives to support people in their own homes is called Carbon Conversations (see chapter 7). This venture has been running for several years and takes place in homes, workplaces and community centres across the UK. It is aimed at people who want support in halving their personal carbon footprint and is done through working with groups of 6-8 people led by a trained volunteer facilitator. Such groups offer a friendly, supportive atmosphere in which participants can explore the different aspects of low-carbon living as it affects their own lives and families. What the group offers participants is:

- *space* for people to explore what climate change means to themselves, their families and their aspirations

- *permission* to share their hopes, fears, doubts and anxieties

- *time* to work through the conflicts between desire, intention, social pressure, status and need

- *reliable*, well-researched information and practical guidance on what will make a difference

- *support* in creating a personal plan for change

The six meetings (see below) use professionally designed materials to cover the basic climate change problem, ideas for a low-carbon future and the four key areas of the footprint - home energy, travel, food and other consumption. Carbon reductions of 1 tonne $CO_2$ are typically made by each member during the course, with plans developed to halve individual footprints over a 4-5 year period.

## The six Carbon Conversation meetings

### 1. Low-carbon futures

Change is tough. It involves letting go of the past and daring to live differently. In this meeting we imagine the futures we want and talk about the journey we're starting.

## 2. Home energy

Home means comfort and safety. It's a place for family and friends. Homes can carry our memories or express our aspirations. But our homes are also a key source of carbon emissions. In this meeting we learn how to make them live up to all our dreams.

## 3. Travel & transport

Car, bike, bus, plane? We use them to get from A to B and each tells a story about who we are: our status and desire. In this meeting we explore what travel means to us and how to gear up for a low-carbon future.

## 4. Food & water

Most people have strong feelings about food - what they like, when to eat, who to share it with and why. In this meeting we explore how to make our diets healthy, enjoyable and low-carbon.

## 5. Consumption & waste

Clothes, gadgets, home improvements, holidays: they all take energy to make and add to our carbon emissions. But they also express who we are, what we value and how we feel. Can we live contentedly with less? This meeting helps us explore some of the most difficult questions about a Western high-consumption lifestyle.

## 6. Moving on

Our final meeting is a reunion. After a few weeks have passed we meet again to celebrate, reflect on learning, share progress, make plans and organise ongoing support.

Source: Carbon Conversations [14]

The *Carbon Conversations Handbook* is the vital backdrop for these meetings and equally valid as a stand-alone resource, indeed one of the best I know of, readable, helpful, authoritative and insightful. Anyone wanting to get to grips with what can be done at home to help create a low-carbon future should look at this.[15]

Home is where it all begins, this life of ours, and we are marked by whatever experiences we may have there, good or bad. This is why what happens at home is so important, they are called our formative years because they do just that, they help form our habits, beliefs, dreams and hopes when younger. I still find myself surprised by some of my father's sayings as I realise how deeply I absorbed them. As a child I often found them boring or even incomprehensible. Now I know just how deeply they came to rest in my psyche and I am grateful for what he taught me - 'If a job is worth doing it is worth doing well'; 'A bad workman always blames his tools'; 'Don't put off till tomorrow what you can do today'. So if you are a parent, aunt, uncle or grandparent, what sort of future do you want for the children in your life? What stories, big and small, do you tell them? What questions do you ask them and what explanations do you give? More than ever we need to be clear about what needs to be challenged, the unsustainable high-carbon story, and what needs to be encouraged, the sustainable low-carbon story. This might be in the literal form of new stories, it may be in the sharing of ideas, it may be in visiting people and projects that exemplify sustainable low-carbon living in practice or, even better, beginning to engage in such activities together - what a challenge, what excitement!

# 11. Learning about sustainability

*One of the tasks of the progressive educator... is to unveil*
*opportunities for hope, no matter what the obstacles may be.*

- Paolo Freire, adult educator[1]

So why is it important, whether you have children or not, to
know something about what goes on in schools? Considering
how much time young people spend there one might hope they
learn quite a bit about sustainability and climate change. So it's
important to know whether that is the case or not in your community. If you are a parent, grandparent or if you work in some
capacity with young people you certainly need to know. If you
are a teacher or governor you should know already. Schools are
well placed to lead in sustainability and climate change matters
and a good number, both primary and secondary, certainly do.
Various terms have been used to describe these concerns in
education (see below). As one may remember from one's own
school days the curriculum is generally described in terms of
subject areas - English, maths, science, geography, history, and
so on - and this largely remains true today. One might also say
this is the traditional story we are told about education, that if
we didn't have distinct subjects where would we be? However, it
is important to know that the way in which we divide up
knowledge varies widely across cultures and across time.

## Joined-up thinking

In chapter 5 reference was made to changing historical world
views and how early developments in science imagined the
world to be like a piece of machinery that could be taken to
pieces and analysed to find out how it worked. Isaac Newton's
discovery of the laws of physics was a case in point. As different

fields of endeavour became identified they were seen as quite different entities from others, physics, chemistry, biology. And at one level they were, but yet still interconnected and part of a whole. Most curriculum subjects today are a reflection of that mechanistic worldview, a separating out of the parts. It enables people to specialise and to become experts in a field. However, as ecologists began to point out in the twentieth-century, in the real world everything is actually connected to everything else. Unless we understand this reality what is knowledge worth? From this understanding came the development of systems thinking, understanding how the parts are interrelated and that the whole is always more than the sum of those parts. The term 'holistic thinking' or 'ecological thinking' are also used when describing the whole system rather than just its different parts.

This idea has also been important in education, especially in primary schools where traditionally one had cross-curricular topics, such as the local area, people that help us or nature and environment. Even in secondary school subjects have sometimes been brought together to demonstrate their interconnections. As a young teacher I was part of a Humanities team run by three subject specialists - English, history and geography. It was challenging, enlightening and exciting. So many issues are cross-curricular, whether citizenship, gender matters, environment or climate change. Some of the terms used today relevant to the concerns of this book are environmental education, global citizenship, education for sustainability, learning for sustainability, climate change education and eco-schools. Users of such terms particularly understand the need for joined-up thinking.

Such thinking is forward-looking rather than traditional in its spirit and, like the low-carbon story, had its origins back in the 1960s and 70s. An enormous amount of work has been done by educators internationally over the last fifty years on environmental issues, sustainability, and more recently climate change. But one may well have missed this depending on when and where one went to school. It is because different political parties and therefore governments have different ideas about what should be in the curriculum. This was not always the case in the UK where teachers, as professionals, were traditionally seen as qualified experts in their field. Under Prime Minister Thatcher in the 80s this all began to change. Politicians, with their differing ideologies, became the alleged experts on education, decreeing what should and should not be in the curriculum. Politicians began to make all the decisions rather than the education profession itself. Broadly, Conservatives favour a more traditional subject-based curriculum whilst Labour has been more open to important cross-curricular themes, such as education for sustainability. The scene is even more varied today with the many types of school that now exist.

## Exemplary award schemes

In order to illustrate what good practice in education for sustainability looks like I have chosen to describe three national award schemes that many schools are involved in - the Ashden Sustainable School Awards, the Food for Life project and Eco-Schools.

## CASE STUDY - The Ashden Awards

These awards were mentioned in chapter 9 and elaborated on in more detail here. Established in 2001, the Ashden Awards are a globally recognised measure of excellence in the field of renewable energy. Awards are given on an annual basis and include a specific category for UK schools. Ashden describes itself as 'a charity that champions and supports the leaders in sustainable energy to accelerate the transition to a low-carbon world'.[2] An account of two 2015 award winning schools is described below.

## *Thornhill Primary School, Cardiff*

### Young eco warriors make big energy savings

Thornhill Primary School's crack squad of student eco-warriors keep energy wastage to a minimum with their spot checks on whether lights and appliances have been left on in the classroom. The school's willingness to trial new ideas and share the results with others, along with its determination to reduce carbon emissions to the absolute minimum, is what makes it the first Welsh school to be a finalist in the Ashden Sustainable School Awards. Solar PV, LED lighting, a building management system and more efficient IT facilities mean that electricity consumption has reduced by over a third since 2011/12. Little wonder that Cardiff City Council use Thornhill as a case study of best practice in carbon reduction.

## *Home Farm Primary School, Colchester*

### Essex Primary School on its very best behaviour

The first primary school in Essex to be awarded a Grade B rating in its Energy Performance Certificate, Home Farm is a model of good behaviour. Between the dream team of Head Teacher Richard Potter and school Business Manager Ceri Stammers, they have managed to turn around a poorly managed heating system and a heat-leaking building to make Home Farm virtually self-sufficient in energy.

The school has an active student Eco-Committee, solar panels on the roof and a new building management system has been installed, all contributing to the impressive turnaround in energy efficiency. One of the simplest yet most productive moves was to enclose a central courtyard which has reduced gas consumption to 60% of what you would expect from a building of this type. The school has also seen a 61% reduction in its electricity use.

Source: Ashden Awards[3]

Ashden supports schools in other ways too and particularly with a year-long scheme called the LESS $CO_2$ Programme. This includes workshops exploring different aspects of energy saving, behaviour change for staff and students and incorporating sustainability into the curriculum. Mentoring is available from Ashden Award-winning schools and an energy audit carried out for each school. The impact so far is: i) 1,000 pupils in forty schools have benefited; ii) 818 tonnes of $CO_2$ emissions have been saved and iii) schools have saved £200,000 on their fuel bills.

## CASE STUDY - Food for Life

Food for Life (FfL) is a national award project set up in 2007 by a number of organisations with a long-standing interest in healthy, tasty and sustainable food. The project's stated brief is to transform food culture in schools and communities.

> Our School Award supports schools to take a whole school approach that sees them grow their own food; organise trips to farms; source food from local producers; set up schools' farmer markets; hold community food events; provide cooking and growing clubs for pupils and their families; serve freshly prepared, well-sourced meals and provide an attractive dining environment so lunchtimes are a positive feature of the school day.[4]

What I like about this project is that it combines all the interrelated parts young people need to know about in order to set food in its wider context. So even the small ones begin by being gardeners, learning about healthy soil and how to grow and look after crops they will later be able to eat. Interested parents and local gardeners may help them with these tasks. Different groups may be responsible for different crops. If there is space this will be in the school grounds, if not in a chosen area nearby. Those who grow food also need to know about cooking food so, often with parental help, this is the next step. Whereas lunch in many schools is an unexciting event here it is made into a positive and lively occasion. Sharing good food together which they have grown themselves brings new meaning, as does getting to know local caterers and farms as well as involving parents and others in the community. This is practical joined-up thinking about food and health which children are not likely to forget. As future parents themselves they may well want to pass this enthusiasm on.

Schools are able to win Food for Life awards at Bronze, Silver and Gold levels, the details of which are summarised below.

### Food for Life: Criteria and Guidance

Food for Life awards are centred around three areas of development, which link to the criteria - creating an action framework for your school:

- Food leadership

- Food quality

- Food culture and community involvement

Here's just a summary of what your school will achieve to get an award at each of the levels.

**BRONZE schools:**

- Serve school meals with seasonal ingredients that are at least 75% freshly prepared

- Involve pupils and parents in planning improvements to school menus and the lunchtime experience, boosting school meal take-up

- Give every pupil the opportunity to visit a local farm, and take part in cooking and food growing activity

**SILVER schools:**

- Serve school meals on proper crockery, not plastic 'flight trays'

- Meet the Silver Food for Life Catering Mark which shows that school food is healthy, ethical, and uses some local and organic ingredients

- Have a cooking club, where pupils get to cook with and eat the produce grown in the school growing area

- Invite parents and the wider community to get involved in food education via food-themed events

- Our food is healthy, ethical and used local ingredients. We use a minimum of 5% organic ingredients in our menus

**GOLD schools:**

- Act as hubs for their local community, actively involving parents and community groups in cooking and growing activities

- Meet the Gold Food for Life Catering Mark which shows the food served is healthy, ethical, uses lots of local ingredients and is animal and climate friendly, including a minimum of 15% organic and 5% free range

- Pupils choosing to eat a school meal is the norm

- Are actively involved in the life of a local farm and active in planning and growing organic food for the school

Source: Food for Life [5]

The work carried out in schools with the support of Food for Life is exemplary in its holistic approach, its involvement with the community and the interest it engenders amongst children and families. It demonstrates what exploration of sustainable food issues can look like at their best.

## CASE STUDY - Eco-Schools

Eco-Schools is an international programme which supports schools in teaching about issues of sustainability through a whole-school approach. It was set up in 1994 and a number of schools in the UK are currently registered with the programme. This requires that schools explore ten main themes which are described below. Whilst brief, taken together the themes provide a comprehensive overview of what learning for sustainability involves and looks like.

### Eco-School Themes

## Biodiversity & nature

Examines the flora and fauna present in the school environment and suggests ways to increase the levels of biodiversity around the school and raises the pupils' awareness of biodiversity and nature.

## Climate change

Examines the impacts we have on the climate through our lifestyles and how our actions can influence the situation in a positive way.

## Energy

Suggests ways in which all members of the school can work together to increase awareness of energy issues and to improve energy efficiency within the school.

## Global citizenship

Examines what our rights and responsibilities are on a national, European and global scale and encourages staff, students and parents to look at the impacts our consumption habits have on other parts of the world.

## Health & wellbeing

Encourages schools to promote the health and wellbeing of young people and the wider community and to make environmental connections to health and safety.

## Litter

Examines the impact of litter on the environment and explores practical means for reducing and minimising the amount of litter produced by the school.

### School grounds

Encourages schools to introduce children to the natural environment and to biodiversity in a practical way by offering a safe and potentially exciting facility for outdoor education that can complement classroom-based activities.

### Transport

Suggests ways for pupils, staff and local government to work together to raise awareness of transport issues and come up with practical solutions that will make a real difference to pupils' everyday lives.

### Waste

Examines the impact of waste on the environment and explores actions to minimise the amount of waste that we produce and dispose of on a daily basis.

### Water

Provides an introduction to the importance of water both locally and globally and raises awareness of how simple actions can substantially cut down water use.

Source: Eco-Schools [6]

In a traditional subject-based curriculum young people learn a lot about the parts (subject areas) but not necessarily about how they contribute to the bigger picture (the whole). The Eco-Schools ten themes were not chosen with school subjects in mind but rather through identifying key issues relating to sustainability and the areas of everyday life in which they occur. Schools approach these themes in different ways depending on the school itself and the age range being taught. What ensures that this is done in a holistic way is the emphasis on a whole-school approach. This means its delivery is not dependent on particular subject areas but is rather an initiative which involves all staff. The steps required for a school to do this effectively are given as follows.

## *Seven steps toward an Eco-School*

### 1: Form an eco-committee

The Eco-Schools Committee is the driving force behind the Eco-Schools process and will represent the ideas of the whole school.

### 2: Carry out an environmental review

Carrying out an environmental review helps the school to identify its current environmental impact and highlights the good, the bad and the ugly.

### 3: Action Plan

The Action Plan is the core of your Eco-Schools work and should be developed using the results of your Environmental Review.

### 4. Monitor and evaluate

To find out whether you are successfully achieving the targets set out in your Action Plan, you must monitor and measure your progress.

### 5. Curriculum work

Besides increasing the status of the programme, linking Eco-School activities to the curriculum ensures that Eco-Schools is truly integrated within the school community.

### 6. Inform and involve

Getting everyone on board! Actions should not just be confined to the school: for example, pupils should take home ideas to put into practice.

### 7: Produce an eco code

A statement that represents the school's commitment to the environment.

### 8: The Green Flag

After at least one year implementing the programme and reaching a high level of performance in complying with these seven steps (sometimes national mandatory criteria also apply), schools can then apply for and be awarded the **Green Flag.** Before receiving their first Green Flag, schools must be assessed by means of a visit, other means of assessment are allowed, although visits are always recommended. Assessment should be carried out on a yearly basis.

Source: Eco-Schools [7]

The Eco-Schools programme is a good example of education for sustainability in action, both in the breadth and interconnectedness of what is taught as well as the whole-school context in which it takes place. The emphasis is on participation, collaboration and empowerment in a way that will affect students' lives in both the present and future.

What these three projects share in common is a holistic approach to learning, which emphasises interconnections and joined-up thinking at all levels. All three deliberately involve all members of the school community and the wider local community. The Ashden Awards focus specifically on the development of low-carbon energy solutions in schools and often with a spin-off in the community. Food for Life takes good food and health as its focus, illustrating how this strand of education for sustainability can empower children, staff and parents. The Eco-Schools programme does the same across the whole curriculum and school ethos. In their shared focus on living more sustainably they illustrate how education in schools can help young people visualise and work towards a more sustainable low-carbon future.

It should be noted, given the role of party politics in UK education, that a change in government always results in changes to the content of the curriculum. Any documentation on what was formerly considered good practice by the departing government quickly disappears from the official records and is replaced by the new government's notion of good practice. At one time, under a Labour government all schools in the UK were encouraged to be eco-schools. Much thought and planning went into this and excellent progress was made in a good number of schools. Like many other sustainability-related issues, this became history under the next incoming Coalition government. One cannot help but feel that matters relating to sustainability and climate change are too important to be excluded from the curriculum on political whim. However, with the freedom many schools now have in relation to the curriculum, education for sustainability could become seen for what it is, the essential core in preparing young people for the shift from a high to a low-carbon economy.

## Good practice in schools

### *Primary*

A good example of materials used in primary schools is Paula Owens' *Little Blue Planet: Investigating spaceship Earth* which contains lesson plans, for use at key stage 1 in primary school, with associated photos and pupil activity sheets. These are specifically intended to help children develop their knowledge about the world - the continents and oceans, maps and globes, oceans, plants, rivers, bees and the planet itself. In explaining why it is important to teach young children about planet Earth the author writes:

> Earth is our home in space, a unique speck in the unimaginably vast cosmos and the only planet in the solar system capable of supporting life as we know it. This little blue planet provides us with all our needs as a species: air to breathe, water to drink, food to eat and an amazing range of resources for clothing, shelter, warmth and succour. However, a good deal of human activity that is concerned with the development and use of these natural resources also threatens our continued existence on this planet. Understanding how, at the simplest level, Earth provides for our needs today and how our actions influence its future bounty (for good and bad), can help young children begin to make informed decisions about the way they live their lives now and in future contexts.[8]

This introduction could have been the opening paragraph of this book. The resource exemplifies good practice in primary school because it introduces children to the notion of 'Spaceship Earth', how it works and why it needs to be respected and looked after. In so doing these lessons create a necessary understanding of the world which underpins appreciation of our wider home and responsibility for its care. It provides an important foundation for later work on social and environmental sustainability.

## *Secondary*

*Hot and Bothered? A study of climate change* is a good example of a resource for GCSE geography. It provides ten lessons for 14-16 year-olds, each of which explores a key question relating to climate change. Each lesson has its own focus: 1. How has climate changed in the past? 2. What is the human impact on climate change? 3. What are the local and global consequences? 4. Could anyone benefit? 5. The USA - Big and bad? 6. Bangladesh - An innocent victim? 7. What exactly are governments doing? 8. How can we change our lifestyles? 9/10. Am I bothered?

One of the activities to help explore changing lifestyles says:

> Hand out post-its on everyday activities that impact on global climate change randomly to pairs of students. Ask them to discuss how people could change their habits or adopt a more environmentally-friendly approach. They must also consider what other social, economic and environmental benefits would result from such changes. When pairs have shared their ideas with the class ask: Which changes would make the most impact on the environment? Which would save households the most money per year? Which would benefit the environment but could be costly to implement? Vote on which changes would be most/least popular.[9]

For further work students can:

> Explore their household's carbon footprint or input the same information into a range of carbon footprint calculators and compare the results. Can they say why the results vary? They can compare the class suggestions for lifestyle changes with those for offsetting carbon emissions on the websites.

Most school work on climate change at secondary level comes under geography or science, although it could be equally explored in literature, biology and art. All these subjects should contribute but since they are distinct Exam Board subjects this is unlikely. In schools which are intentionally holistic such linkages would be much more possible. Some of the key questions one would expect children to be exploring overall are shown below.

Asking the right questions about changing climate

## *Sixth form*

In response to an article I wrote on 'A post-carbon geography' I was contacted by Tom Deacon, who works for the Field Studies Council (FSC).[10] This organisation aims to 'bring environmental understanding to all' and has a number of centres around the country which provide courses for individuals, schools, colleges and families. In a nutshell FSC believes that 'the more we understand about and take inspiration from the world around us the more we can appreciate its needs and protect its diversity and beauty for future generations.'[11] What Tom contacted me about was the design of a new A-level Geography fieldwork course. What interested him and the exam board was the opportunity to include exploration of carbon and post-carbon futures as part of fieldwork.

The draft section on 'Carbon, climate and the future' reads:

> Understanding and acting on carbon and climate change are as much social issues, involving beliefs and attitudes, as they are technical or scientific. To recognise and act on this societally is the challenge faced by current and future generations around the planet we share. As geographers this crosses all aspects of our discipline and calls for interdisciplinary collaboration. At a local scale this means exploring the role of communities and individuals, as well as organisations and policy makers in this move towards a post-carbon future.
>
> Focusing on an urban setting learners will investigate societal carbon and its implications for climate change, visioning a sustainable post-carbon future. Learners will carry out fieldwork in a local settlement, mapping carbon in the form of transport, energy and consumption and exploring opportunities for climate change mitigation in urban settings. Learners will set out a vision for a positive post-carbon future for the settlement - outlining necessary mitigation and adaptation through exploring the players, pathways, values and their own involvement in this process.
>
> Climate Cycle draft [12]

What exciting possibilities lie ahead for 6th form geographers in their fieldwork and what better preparation for a low-carbon future.

The examples given here of what can go on in schools provide a flavour of what is happening in the UK. I have taken geography as an example because it is one area where issues of sustainability and climate change occur in the curriculum. There will be others and not just within geography.

## *Tensions and debates*

There is a proviso that needs to be made about the analysis made in relation to issues of sustainability. This debate occurs amongst educators but is also relevant more widely in society. It is sometimes described as the difference between 'light green' and 'dark green' perspectives on environmental matters. Earlier chapters made it clear that issues to do with the state of the environment are the subject of much discussion and argument. This often centres around two main issues, how tricky/difficult/bad things actually are (social, environmental, economic) and the degree of adjustment needed to stabilise/improve/resolve things (Does it require surface or deep change?). So, whether it's about what one teaches or what one says in the pub, these distinctions really do matter. How bad do I think things are and how deep do the changes need to be? At one end of the spectrum is: there are some problems that need sorting but we can resolve them in the usual ways. At the other end is: there are major problems which we cannot possibly resolve in the usual way. In terms of future scenarios the first view is known as 'light green', the problems are acknowledged and seen as difficult but resolvable. This tends to lead to a business-as-usual scenario, where existing techniques and procedures are used as before in order to resolve the problem. The second view is known as 'dark green', because the problems are seen as more serious and potentially unresolvable, unless major change takes place. This analysis arises from the view that it is our very way of life (social, economic, political) that caused the problems in the first place. Tinkering with the old high-carbon system will not resolve things (shallow change). Creating a new low-carbon system (deep change) can begin to help resolve things in that it's based on the notion of sustainability and climate change mitigation and adaptation.

## Education for transition

However we look at it there will be turbulent times as we do/don't reject the old high-carbon story and do/don't accept the new low-carbon story. It will be a long social, economic, political and cultural transition that affects all of us. Here are some suggestions as to what the key elements of education for such a transition might look like.

### *Some key elements*

#### 1. **The 'long transition'**

How this came about, its main features and the problems it throws up. The goals of a low-carbon transition, how it can work and how the notion can go viral.

#### 2. **Climate change**

The nature and origins of changing climate, its past, present and future impacts and forms of mitigation and adaptation required in the local community.

#### 3. **Energy issues**

Understanding the nature and origins of the high-carbon story, its contribution to climate change and the wider consequences for society of fossil-fuel addiction.

#### 4. **Low-carbon**

The need for each community to consider its current use of fossil fuel and to plan for a future which will use less energy and is also low-carbon.

#### 5. **Psychology of change**

Ways of acknowledging and working positively with feelings of despair, pain, grief and loss, including post-petroleum distress disorder.

## 6. **Positive visions**

Learning to work with a diversity of people in one's local community to envision and plan the changes needed to create a low-carbon community.

## 7. **Cultural stories**

Letting go of the old cultural story of domination and consumerism and replacing this with new eco-centred stories of more just and sustainable futures.

## 8. **Systems thinking**

Learning to see and experience relationships and society as nested within nature/the biosphere and adapting one's life accordingly to this.

## 9. **Building resilience**

Ensuring that each community can look after more of its own needs and that it has slack in the system so as to recover more easily when faced with problems.

## 10. **Localisation**

Understanding that a sustainable low-carbon world will need to work both from the bottom up and the top down so that needs are met more locally.

## 11. **Case studies**

Learning from various initiatives about what sustainability in practice looks like, from issues such as food, building and transport to energy and biodiversity.

## 12. **Starting up**

Learning all the new skills needed in order to play one's part in this transition and passing them on in turn to those who come after.

Source: Author [13]

For more in-depth study of low-carbon sustainable futures you will find *Sustainable Schools, Sustainable Futures* [13] and *Educating for Hope in Troubled Times: Climate change and the transition to a post-carbon future* useful sources.[14] Overall this chapter has looked at the importance of education in different contexts and shared examples of good practice relevant to education for sustainability and climate change. It has raised questions about how knowledge is artificially divided up and the vital need for systemic joined-up thinking as well as what is or isn't going on in your local schools. Are the children you know being prepared for a future that will be very different from today?

# 12. Creating low-carbon community

*What we are convinced of is this: If we wait for the governments, it's too little, too late. If we act as individuals, it'll be too little. But if we act as communities, it might just be enough, just in time.*

Rob Hopkins, founder of Transition Movement[1]

Whilst chapter 10 focused on home and household it was not intended to suggest that responding to climate change as individuals is enough on its own. It was however suggesting that we all individually have a role to play. The question, 'What can one person do on their own?' is often used as an excuse for doing nothing. Quite clearly many people doing things will achieve more. The previous chapter highlighted the significant achievements that are possible when the school as a community puts its mind to things. More can be achieved than the sum of the parts. The next step is to ask what low-carbon activities are going on or could be going on in one's street, suburb, village, parish or town. Change of any sort is more likely to come about when people become concerned at grassroots level and this is the local community, however one chooses to describe it.

For millennia the local community meant the place that was home, where one supported and was supported by others. Of course people also wanted to see the world and sometimes moved to other communities. In the last two hundred years there have been many movements and migrations across the globe, communities have become more culturally rich and diverse. In the last fifty years older people have watched that sense of community disappear as individualism and consumerism increasingly hold sway. But in the great transition from high to low-carbon communities which is now beginning to occur we need all the support possible to achieve this goal. It is not just about homes and schools but businesses, shops, workplaces, services, voluntary organisations, councils and others that need to work out what their contribution is and how they can support the community in this shift.

Each sector of the community needs to grasp the three-fold nettle of accountability: firstly, acknowledging their own responsibility for climate change in the community; secondly, identifying their particular contribution to climate change adaptation and mitigation; and thirdly, building a vital community network of sharing, inspiration and committed action. In the same way as this book has been about bringing threads together, so communities must also do this in their search for a safer, healthier and more secure future. The first task is to monitor what is already going on locally in the field of sustainability and low-carbon living, beginning to join up the dots. Who is already engaged in these matters, who are the workers, mentors, helpers and champions in your local community? Three vital threads will be explored here: i) the need to make carbon more visible in the community so everyone can see and understand how the links in the high-carbon chain operate; ii) the need to identify and gather existing examples of good practice and expertise in the community and elsewhere; iii) the need to thus create a community which is more cohesive and resilient in the face of hazards to come.

## Seeing climate change

A valuable resource on developing local solutions referred to previously is Stephen Sheppard's *Visualizing Climate Change*.[2] Sheppard argues that one of the key tasks is to develop carbon consciousness and carbon literacy, that is for individuals and communities to become more visually aware of high-carbon at work in their local area, since once something is made visible it becomes easier to tackle. Communities too need to see climate change causes, impacts, adaptation and mitigation as an interacting whole system. Sometimes we see the evidence on a regular basis but may not identify it as having anything to do with a high-carbon lifestyle. So how does one go looking for this visual evidence? Sometimes it's in front of our noses, in the media or on social networks. Offshore oil rigs are one place where the carbon chain begins and also fossil-fired power stations which generate our electricity. Every petrol or diesel vehicle on the road, plastic products and lights and computers left on, all represent carbon in the community. Once we start labelling features such as these 'high-carbon' the clearer the links that criss-cross our communities become.

Much of what we thought was just variable weather over the last two decades has actually been the impact of climate change: torrential rain and flooding, spring coming earlier, ornamental trees flowering twice. Similarly, one may see examples of adaptation and limitation without recognising them for what they are. This would include rooftop solar panels, solar farms and wind farms, new sea defences and beach restoration. Whilst backyard vegetable plots, community gardens and farmers' markets have been around for some time they are increasingly a response to a high-carbon food footprint. More energy efficient buildings, electric vehicles, cycling and walking are also manifestations of low-carbon activity. So there is an alphabet, as it were, both of the old high-carbon story and the newly emerging low-carbon story in our communities.

Once we begin to see these features for what they are and understand the part they play in our locality it is much easier to confront or support them. As explained in chapter 4 there are all sorts of reasons why a carbon cover-up occurs. Seeing, recognising and understanding are the first steps in climate literacy and from this can come more conversation and discussion in the community. Once out in the open the issue is then also heard in households, schools, workplace, pubs and bus stops. From this recognition it becomes more possible to share one's concerns, make caring a public norm and action with others a convivial possibility. It's not just me on my own, it's us together.

## Engaging with the transition

The whole experience of being part of a major social, cultural and historic transition from high to low-carbon living may last for many decades and it will necessarily bring up all sorts of feelings. These may range from feeling challenged, excited and full of energy to troubled, wary and undecided. As we have seen previously part of the answer is to be working with like-minded others who can support you, thus the emphasis on action in and with the community. All communities, whatever their size, inevitably bring together local people with similar interests. Some groups will be connected to similar initiatives elsewhere in the county, country or internationally. The Transition Network is a good example of what can occur when people begin to flag up locally a concern about climate change, energy costs, environmental concerns or the state of the economy.[3] Transition groups begin with a group of friends or neighbours who want to find others to share their thoughts with. When people begin to do this it is likely a diversity of interests will be present, from energy, ecology and food to transport, health and well-being.

Over nearly a decade now many such groups have sprung up across the world with a common interest in moving from a high to a low-carbon lifestyle and economy. Many of them describe themselves as Transition groups and are part of a loosely affiliated international network, the Transition Network. There are also innumerable other groups concerned about climate change, economic inequality, environmental damage and a more sustainable future. Transition groups are often noted for their inventiveness in raising awareness of issues locally and globally and using their communities as a seedbed for change. Over a number of years the Network has identified the key principles which have emerged from its work. Here are some of them.

# CASE STUDY - Some Transition Network principles

## 1. Positive visioning

- We can only create what we can first vision. If we can't imagine a positive future we won't be able to create it.

- Change is happening - our choice is between a future we want and one which happens to us. The generation of new stories and myths are central to this visioning work.

## 2. Help people access good information and trust them to make good decisions

- Transition initiatives dedicate themselves to raising awareness of peak oil and climate change and related issues such as critiquing economic growth. They recognise the responsibility to present this information in ways which are playful, articulate, accessible and engaging, and which enable people to feel enthused and empowered rather than powerless.

- Transition initiatives focus on telling people the closest version of the truth that we know in times when the information available is deeply contradictory.

## 3. Inclusion and openness

- Successful Transition initiatives need an unprecedented coming together of the broad diversity of society. They dedicate themselves to ensuring that their decision-making processes and their working groups embody principles of openness and inclusion.

- This principle also refers to the principle of each initiative reaching the community in its entirety and endeavouring, from an early stage, to engage their local business community, the diversity of community groups and local authorities.

## 4. **Enable sharing and networking**

- Transition initiatives dedicate themselves to sharing their successes, failures, insights and connections at the various scales across the Transition network, so as to more widely build up a collective body of experience.

## 5. **Build resilience**

- This stresses the fundamental importance of building resilience, that is, the capacity of our businesses, communities and settlements to deal as well as possible with shock.

- Transition initiatives commit to building resilience across a wide range of areas (food, economics, energy etc) and also on a range of scales (from the local to the national) as seems appropriate - and to setting them within an overall context of the need to do all we can to ensure general environmental resilience.

## 6. **Inner *and* outer transition**

- The impact of the information about the state of our planet can generate fear and grief - which may underlie the state of denial that many people are caught in.

- This principle also honours the fact that Transition thrives because it enables and supports people to do what they are passionate about, what they feel called to do.

## 7. **Transition makes sense - the solution is the same size as the problem**

- Many films or books suggest that changing light bulbs, recycling and driving smaller cars may be enough. This causes a state called 'cognitive dissonance' - a trance where you have been given an answer, but know that it is not going to solve the problem you've just been given.

- We look at the whole system not just one issue because we are facing a systems failure not a single problem failure.

From: Transition Network [4]

There is much food for thought here and further explanation and discussion of the full principles can be found on the Transition Network website. Also of immediate interest here are examples of practical projects in action. Wide-ranging examples are reported regularly on the Transition Network website and an example is given below. This comes from a report by Rob Hopkins, founder of the Transition Network, on his visit to a French commune, the village of Ungersheim in Alsace. A commune in France is an official administrative division roughly equal to a township.

## Ungersheim, a Village in Transition

I am often asked the question what it might look like if a local government really took Transition by the horns, initiated it, and acted as the catalyst for the community to start a meaningful and impactful Transition process. Having visited Ungersheim in the Alsace region of eastern France, I can now tell you exactly what it looks like.

I was invited by Ungersheim's remarkable Mayor, Jean-Claude Mensch and the Commune d'Ungersheim to speak at their 'Les Rencontres de la Transition' event (Meetings of Transition) and to see what they have been doing there. Several years ago, Mensch hosted a visit by an organisation called the General Assembly of the Citizens of the World, at which the film *'In Transition 1.0'* was screened. It led to a conversation in the Commune along the lines of 'We're already doing that, let's become a Transition town'. And so they did.

They are the first Transition initiative I know of to be launched by a local authority in this way. Ungersheim is a village with a population of around 2,000, and is a place with a long history of mining. At its peak, the extraction of potash, used to make potassium for agricultural use and sodium chloride (salt) for treating ice on roads, employed 13,000 people in the region. The last mine closed in 2003. In France, mayors have a lot more power than they do in other parts of the world, so it is fascinating to see just what can be achieved when a mayor is inspired by Transition. Here are some of the things that have already been done in Ungersheim.

o   Introduced more participative democracy

o   Mapped the biodiversity of the area in an 'Atlas of Biodiversity'

o   Installed a wood biomass boiler to heat the swimming pool

o   Built a 5.3MW solar installation and industrial estate

o   All public lighting low energy bulbs and 40% reduction in energy use

o   Assessed all public buildings for their energy consumption

o   Completely banned all pesticides and herbicides in public areas

o   Changed catering at local primary school to 100% organic meals

o   Transformed 8 hectares of land into an organic market

o   This provides 250 baskets of food for families each week

From: Rob Hopkins blog [5]

## Growing resilience

When communities are faced with new situations, such as the impacts of climate change and faltering economies, all sorts of stresses and strains become apparent in the struggle to catch up with unforeseen change and adjustment to the new 'normal' it brings in its wake. When disequilibrium occurs in any system, whether ecological or human, it is faced with the issue of resilience. Resilience in this context has been defined as 'the ability to adapt to change and continue not only to function, but also to thrive. In a world challenged by climate change and limited availability of non-renewable resources, a focus on resilience is sustainability in its broadest sense'.[6] Jacqui Hodgson and Rob Hopkins develop this further.

> Responding to each of these new energy, climate, and economic 'normals' will require one common strategy: *building community resilience*. Efforts that build community resilience enhance our ability to navigate the energy, climate, and economic crises of the 21st century. Done right, they can also serve as the foundation of a whole new economy - an economy comprised of people and communities that thrive within the real limits of our beautiful but finite planet...Thankfully, innovations that build community resilience are cropping up everywhere, and in many forms: community-owned, distributed, renewable energy production; sustainable local food systems; new cooperative business models; sharing economies, re-skilling and more.[7]

Working together to help create low-carbon community

In the past, only a generation or two ago, most communities possessed the basic skills that were needed for daily life such as growing and preserving their own food, the making of clothes and repairing and building homes with local materials. Some of those skills, ones which our grandparents and great-grandparents would have taken more for granted, are still around in specialist contexts and there are people still devoted to the maintenance of these crafts, which may well be needed again.

Some of those concerned about the transition from a high to low-carbon society talk about the need for communities to create their own 'energy descent action plan'. This is based on acknowledging that use of fossil fuels must be phased out as soon as possible to be replaced by locally generated renewable energy. This has to include a reduction in the amount we use overall, in short a more sustainable approach to energy. One of the first examples of such a plan is *Transition in Action: Totnes and District 2030*.[8] Three assumptions underpin this plan: firstly, that oil and other fossil fuels need to be left in the ground; secondly, that climate change is growing apace and we can no longer afford to procrastinate; thirdly, that endless economic growth is no longer possible or feasible. Whether governments play a significant part in facilitating the transition or not it would seem that it will be a bumpy ride as we have to face up to more extreme weather conditions, ongoing economic problems, probably with intermittent energy supply and possibly food shortages.

> Central to this is resilience. Resilience is, in a nutshell, the ability of a system, whether an individual, an economy, a town or a city, to withstand shock from the outside. As the credit crunch highlighted, the global economy is now so highly networked, that a shock or crisis in one part can pulse very fast through the rest of the system. Resilience is about building the ability to adapt to shock, to flex and modify, rather than crumble. You can think of it as being like building surge protectors into an electrical system.[9]

The Totnes Descent Plan begins with a reflection on the town's recent past between 1930 and 1960 as an important and thriving market town. Food was a much more local affair with people growing some of their own fruit and vegetables and buying other foodstuffs, often grown locally, from local shops. Until the 1950s the town was powered mainly by 'town gas', made from local coal. Whilst the economy also partly depended on products from other parts of the UK and the world, towns such as Totnes were much more self-reliant than today because their support system was more local and flexible. There was also much more of an ethos of 'make do and mend' so that items were more easily repaired and therefore had a longer life than in today's throwaway society.

After this historical review of a time when the town was more self-reliant, the report sets out the initiatives introduced since the inception of Transition Totnes in 2005. These actions have been wide ranging, from food security, water, farming, biodiversity and energy to transport, building and economics. Focusing then on future needs an energy descent plan was drawn up for the period 2009-2030. Central to this was a widespread and inclusive process of community engagement. I've taken this example to highlight some of the different aspects that need to be considered when exploring issues of community resilience. Paramount here is the ability of local organisations to work together in an inclusive way towards common low-carbon goals.

A network is resilient when it has slack in the system, spare capacity, alternative back-up routes and can thus respond creatively to whatever surprises and dangers it is faced with. It is about having a creative emergency plan for all eventualities, but it is also about having a back-up plan for when any of those fail. It is always worth thinking about the unthinkable because it often has an irritating habit of catching us unawares. At its most basic a community needs to know how it can continue to function effectively when any or several of the following systems are malfunctioning: energy supply, food supply, health support, safe shelter. It has been argued for example that blackouts are more likely to occur in the future, as a result of extreme weather, irregular energy supply or old and outdated distribution systems. In the past decade China, Brazil and Italy have all had significant power failures. Similarly, hiccups in the global food chain, whether from climate related crop damage or transportation difficulties, would soon empty supermarket shelves. We need to become more resilient both at home and in our communities.

Whilst the notion of the need for resilience is central to transition thinking this concept has also been widely embraced in a variety of other social contexts.[10] I see the wider use of resilience as a concept to be a reflection of the times we live in - fast changing, uncertain, troubled, unhealthy, turbulent and dangerous, even without climate change. To survive in such times we need to be alert, insightful, prepared and, yes, resilient. The term can of course also be used in a weak or relatively meaningless way as was discussed in relation to the notion of sustainability in chapter 3.

## Affirming the future

We are all interested in, cautious about or hopeful for the future. It is time that has yet to come and when it arrives it is no longer the future but the now. Time that is 'not yet', time that is still to come, because of its lack of immediate presence can act as a screen on which to project our hopes and fears - long life and good health, grandchildren yet to be born, the success we've always sought in our field. What is sometimes called futures thinking - the ability to look ahead, weigh up the possible impact of actions, make choices and take steps to create the future you need - is a vital element in the human condition.

We are future-orientated animals because we are able to project ourselves into future time and reflect on what we may find there. We can and should also do this for others, not least our children and grandchildren, if one has them, but also on behalf of all those as yet unborn. What sort of future did your parents want you to have? What actions did they take and sacrifices make on your behalf? Everything we do influences both the present and future, sometimes in small ways but also in large ways too. We do not necessarily know what the outcomes of those decisions will be, but we make them in good faith and because we believe right actions matter and can make a difference.

There are economists, philosophers and lawyers who have raised the question as to what the rights of future generations might be or indeed, since they are as yet unborn, whether they have any at all. Over the years there has been a growing consensus that even as we expect to have rights, so also should future generations. This principle is known as intergenerational justice. If we ask whose responsibility it is to protect those needs the answer has to be *us*, the present generation. A sustainable low-carbon economy would therefore be one which meets the needs of current society without compromising the ability of future generations to meet their needs too. It is therefore argued that no generation should inherit less human and natural wealth than the one that came before it. Such rights are not yet enshrined in international law but what is clear is that all sorts of national and international NGOs (non-governmental organisations), with interests ranging from climate, environment and justice to poverty, peace and hunger are working to help create a fairer, safer and more just society. All of those who hold some notion of a better world have a particular interest in creating a better future, whether for their community, country or planet.

In my younger days the nuclear arms race between America and the Soviet Union seemed likely to result in nuclear war, but it didn't, although it came extremely close. What then looked like the probable future was averted. The dilemma with climate change is that it cannot be averted although comprehensive local and international mitigation can limit its impact. If the deniers and sceptics (see chapter 6) had been swiftly sidelined in the 1980s action could have been taken sooner by governments to avert the carbon excesses of the last thirty years.

There is a new wave of thinking and seeing that more and more people are being drawn to across the world. This is not merely wishful thinking but observed and recorded actuality.[11] Whilst the emphasis may differ, at heart this is about the need to live more sustainably in one's place in ways that do less rather than more harm to people and biosphere. The other side of the coin is the obligation to resist all that which causes harm and damage to people and planet, confronting and rejecting those principles and procedures which lead to unsustainable and harmful practice. In this Companion I have focused on the hazards of global heating and climate change, not because I see them as any more important than issues of conflict, inequality or human rights, but because they threaten the planet we live on, which is home. In these times a sustainable low-carbon future is both necessity and luxury.

# Postscript: After Paris

As I finished drafting this book in 2015 the UN Conference on Climate Change in Paris achieved what many called a 'landmark deal'. Here are the key points of that deal.

- 195 countries agreed we should aim to limit the increase in average global temperature to well below 2C and preferably 1.5C
- All countries agreed that they would voluntarily cut their own carbon emissions
- The longer term aim is to reduce carbon emissions to zero by the middle of the century
- From 2020 wealthier countries will support developing countries in adapting to climate change
- The combined pledges so far to cut carbon emissions will not be enough to keep warming below 2C, so every five years these pledges will be ramped up
- There is a mechanism to take into account the loss and damage caused to the most vulnerable countries
- What is called the 'Paris Agreement' will come into force in 2020

For 195 people, let alone that number of countries, to come to an agreement on such a complex topic could be seen as a miracle, but a necessary one. The devil lies in the detail. What is it that the agreement leaves out? Much of the final document is an important statement of principle, the key ideas that need to underpin existing and future adaptation and mitigation practices. What disappointed many was that the national carbon reduction figures are voluntary, that is left to each country to decide for itself. Some countries have such figures enshrined in law. Others plan cuts which some would consider inadequate, so this is politically a delicate area for debate. It is to be hoped that the five-year review of such pledges will encourage on-going faster and deeper cuts.

These cuts will depend on governments and their electorates constantly striving to move away from the high-carbon story and towards a cleaner and safer low-carbon economy. I therefore find it curious that in the months leading up to the Paris conference the UK government was moving in the opposite direction. I say this because prior to the conference these are the low-carbon initiatives the UK Conservative government had chosen to cut: i) scrapping support for onshore wind; ii) axing subsidies for solar power; iii) removing subsidies for fossil fuel power stations that want to convert to wood or biomass; iv) ending subsidies to homeowners wanting to install better insulation and energy efficient boilers; v) selling off most of the green investment bank set up in 2012 to help green projects; vi) removing low car taxation for electric and hybrid vehicles; vii) dropping the plan for promoting zero-carbon homes; ix) allowing fracking to take place in important nature sites. If this deliberate turn around and walking away from the Paris accord wasn't so serious it would read like something from a black farce. This is why one needs to keep a sharp eye on what politicians are doing, or not doing, in relation to the global low-carbon shift that all countries in the world now recognise as essential to our safety.

There is also much to take heart from. For example, the International Energy Agency reports that globally nearly half of all the new power plants in 2014 use renewable sources of energy, now a mainstream fuel, a clear sign the energy transition is under way. In the UK most of Britain's largest cities are likely to run on renewables by 2050 after council leaders pledged to cut carbon emissions. This will result in greener transport, the end of gas heating and widespread insulation of homes. The cities include Edinburgh, Manchester, Newcastle, Liverpool, Leeds, Nottingham and Glasgow. Action for low-carbon change is beginning to occur at all levels of society. That is why this Companion focuses, in particular, on what *we* can do in our families and communities when working with like-minded others. We are the ones called upon to make the difference. There is no 'someone else' who is going to sort everything out for us, but there are millions of others working towards similar low-carbon and sustainable outcomes. These are our allies, whether family, neighbours, friends or colleagues and whatever community or country they may live in. We are not alone.

# Sources

## Chapter 1: What do we need to know?

1.  Hulme, M. (2009) *Why We Disagree About Climate Change*, Cambridge University Press (p.v)
2.  Thatcher, M. (1988) Speech to the Royal Society. Online. www.margaretthatcher.org/document/107346
3.  Sheppard, S. (2012) *Visualising Climate Change: A guide to visual communication of climate change and developing local solutions*, Routledge
4.  King, Sir David (2014) Transition Network. Online. www.transitionnetwork.org/blogs/rob-hopkins/2014-04/sir-david-king-climate-change-biggest-diplomatic-challenge-all-time
5.  Klein, N. (2015) *This Changes Everything: Capitalism vs the climate*, Penguin
6.  Vince, G. (2014) *Adventures in the Anthropocene: A journey to the heart of the planet we made*, Chatto & Windus
7.  Orr, D. (1994) *Earth in Mind: On education, environment and the human prospect*, Island Press (p.112)

## Chapter 2: What's energy got to do with it?

1.  Buchan, D. (2010) *The Rough Guide to the Energy Crisis*, Rough Guides (p.vi)
2.  Goldenberg, S. (2013) Just 90 companies caused two-thirds of man-made global warming emissions, *Guardian, The*, 20 Nov. Online. www.theguardian.com/environment/2013/nov/20/90-companies-man-made-global-warming-emissions-climate-change
3.  Carrington, D. (2015) Leave fossil fuels buried to prevent climate change, study urges, *The Guardian*, January 7

4. Fossil Free UK (2015). Online. http://gofossilfree.org/uk/
5. Boyle, G. (201) *Renewable Energy: Power for a sustainable future*, 3rd edition, Oxford University Press
6. UK Committee on Climate Change (2013) *Fourth Carbon Budget Review*, UKCCC
7. Worldwatch Institute (2014) *Vital Signs: The trends that are shaping our future*, Volume 21, Island Press
8. Nathan, S. (2007) Stephen Salter: pioneer of wave power, *The Engineer* . Online. www.theengineer.co.uk/in-depth/stephen-salter-pioneer-of-wave-power/299034.article
9. International Energy Association (2015) Online. www.iea.org/topics/renewables/
10. UK Department of Energy and Climate Change (2014) DECC Public Attitudes Tracker - Wave 10: Summary of findings. Online. www.gov.uk/government/uploads/system/uploads/attachment_data/file/342426/Wave_10_findings_of_DECC_Public_Attitudes_Tracker_FINAL.pdf
11. Hicks, D. (2014) *Educating for Hope in Troubled Times: Climate change and the transition to a post-carbon future*, Institute of Education Press
12. Urry, J. (2013) *Societies Beyond Oil: Oil dregs and social futures*, Zed Books (p.210)
13. Urry, J. (2013) *Societies Beyond Oil*, Zed Books (p.215)
14. Heinberg, R. (2005) *The Party's Over: Oil, war and the fate of industrial societies*, Clairview Books

## Chapter 3: What's the choice of futures

1. Turney, J. (2010) *The Rough Guide to the Future*, Rough Guides (p.vi)
2. Worldwatch Institute (2014) *Vital Signs: The trends that are shaping our future*, Island Press
3. Hutton, W. (2015) *How Good We Can Be: Ending the mercenary society and building a great country*, Little, Brown

4. Engleman, R. (2015) Beyond sustainababble, chapter 1 in: The Worldwatch Institute, *State of the World 2015*, Worldwatch Institute (p.3)
5. Carson, R. (1962) *Silent Spring*, Penguin Classics (2000)
6. Meadows, D.H., Meadows, D.L., Randers, R. and Behrens, W. (1974) *The Limits to Growth*, Pan Books
7. Visser, W. (2009)*The Top Fifty Sustainability Books*, Cambridge University Press
8. Folke, C. (2013) Respecting planetary boundaries and reconnecting to the biosphere, chapter 2 in: Assadourian, E. and Prugh, T. (eds) *State of the World 2013: Is sustainability still possible?* Island Press (p.19)
9. Mabey, R. (2010) *A Brush With Nature: 25 years of personal reflection on the natural world*, BBC Books
10. Happy Planet Index (2015) Online. www.happyplanetindex.org
11. Wilkinson, R. and Pickett, K. (2009) *The Spirit Level: Why more equal societies almost always do better*, Allen Lane
12. Leonard, A. (2010) *The Story of Stuff*, Constable & Robinson
13. Washington, H. (2015) *Demystifying Sustainability: Towards real solutions*, Earthscan/Routledge (p.195)

## Chapter 4: The old story: high-carbon

1. Berry, T. (1988)*The Dream of the Earth*, Sierra Club Books (p.123)
2. Meighan, R. and Harber, C. (2007) *A Sociology of Educating*, Continuum (p.212) (5th edition)
3. Osborne, R. (2014) *Iron, Steam and Money: The making of the Industrial Revolution*, Pimlico (p.345)
4. Lawson, N. (2009) *All Consuming: How shopping got us into this mess and how we can find our way out*, Penguin (p.2)
5. Leonard, A. (2010) *The Story of Stuff*, Constable

6.  Greer, J.M. (2015) *After Progress: Reason and religion at the end of the Industrial Age*, New Society Publishers (pp.37-8)
7.  Hutton, W. (2015) *How Good Can We Be: Ending the mercenary society and building a great country*, Little, Brown

## Chapter 5: The new story: low-carbon

1.  Lao Tzu, Chinese philosopher and poet, 6th century BC
2.  Meadows, D., Randers, J., Meadows, D. (2005) *Limits to Growth: The 30-year update*, Earthscan
3.  Roszac, T. (1968/1995) *The Making of a Counter Culture*, University of California Press
4.  Roszac, T. (1978/2003) *Person/Planet: The creative disintegration of industrial society*, iUniverse Inc. (p.xix)
5.  Capra, F. (1982) *The Turning Point: Science, society, and the rising culture*, Bantam Books. See also Capra, F. and Luisi, P. (2015) *The Systems View of Life: A unifying vision*, Cambridge University Press
6.  Bohm, D. (1983) *Wholeness and the Implicate Order*, Ark Paperbacks, Routledge & Kegan Paul (p.112)
7.  Sterling, S. (2009) Ecological intelligence: viewing the world relationally, in Stibbe, A. (ed) *The Handbook of Sustainability Literacy: Skills for a changing world*, Green Books (p.77-83)
8.  Judt, T. (2010) *Ill Fares the Land: A treatise on our present discontents*, Allen Lane
9.  Boyle, G. ed. (2012) *Renewable Energy: Power for a Sustainable Future*, 3rd edition, Oxford University Press
10. Earth Overshoot Day. Online. www.footprintnetwork.org/en/index.php/GFN/page/earth_overshoot_day
11. Global Footprint Network (2015). Online. www.footprintnetwork.org
12. Farming Futures. Online. www.farmingfutures.org.uk

13. WWF (2014) *Living Planet Report 2014.* Online. www.wwf.eu/media_centre/publications/living_planet_r eport/
14. Wellbeing of Future Generations Bill (2015) https://your.caerphilly.gov.uk/communityplanning/sites /your.caerphilly.gov.uk/communityplanning/files/future _generations_bill_report_15_.pdf

## Chapter 6: Feeling the way forward

1. Australian Psychological Society (2015) Climate change what you can do. Online. www.psychology.org.au/publications/tip_sheets/climate/
2. Norgaard, K. (2011) *Living in Denial: Climate change, emotions and everyday life*, MIT Press
3. Randall, R. and Brown, A. (2015) *In Time for Tomorrow? The Carbon Conversations Handbook*, Surefoot Effect (p.11)
4. *New Scientist* (2010) State of denial: a special report, 15 May
5. Oreskes, N. and Conway, E. (2010) *Merchants of Doubt: How a handful of scientists obscured the truth on issues from tobacco smoke to global warming*, Bloomsbury
6. Macy, J. and Johnstone, C. (2012) *Active Hope: How to face the mess we're in without going crazy*, New World Library
7. Carbon Conversations (2015) Online. At www.carbonconversations.org/what-carbon-conversations
8. Sander, J. and Conway, P. (2013) Think Global Thinkpiece: Psychological approaches within sustainable and global learning. Online. http://think-global.org.uk/resources/item/7531

9. Clayton, S., Manning, C.M., and Hodge, C. (2014) Beyond storms and droughts: The psychological impacts of climate change, American Psychological Association and ecoAmerica (p.34) Online. http://ecoamerica.org/wp-content/uploads/2014/06/eA_Beyond_Storms_and_Drou ghts_Psych_Impacts_of_Climate_Change.pdf
10. Hicks, D. (2014) *Educating for Hope in Troubled Times: Climate change and transition to a post-carbon future*, Institute of Education Press
11. Macy, J. and Johnstone, C. (2012) *Active Hope: How to face the mess we're in without going crazy*, New World Library

## Chapter 7: Getting things done

1. Hayward, B, (2012) *Children, Citizenship and Environment: Nurturing a democratic imagination in a changing world*, Routledge (p.152)
2. Music, G. (2012) *The Good Life: Wellbeing and the new science of altruism, selfishness and morality*, Routledge (p.3)
3. Hayward, B, (2012) *Children, Citizenship and Environment: Nurturing a democratic imagination in a changing world*, Routledge (p.21)
4. Klein, N. (2015) *This Changes Everything: Capitalism vs the climate*, Penguin
5. Birdwell, J. and Bani, B. (2014) 'Today's teenagers are more engaged with social issues than ever...' Introducing Generation Citizen, London: DEMOS (p.1)
6. Birdwell, J. and Bani, B. (2014) 'Today's teenagers are more engaged with social issues than ever...' Introducing Generation Citizen, London: DEMOS
7. Randall, R. and Brown, A. (2015) *In Time for Tomorrow? The Carbon Conversations Handbook*, The Surefoot Effect
8. Randall, R. and Brown, A. (2015) *In Time for Tomorrow? The Carbon Conversations Handbook*, The Surefoot Effect (p.49)

9. Hopkins, R. (2015) *21 Stories of Transition*, Transition Network (p.19)
10. Macfadyen, P. (2015) *Flatpack Democracy: A DIY guide to creating independent politics*, Bath: eco-logic books (p.3)

## Chapter 8: Adapting to climate change

1. Benjamin Franklin, Founding Father of the United States
2. *Guardian, The* (2015) Majority of Britons worried about global warming, poll finds, 4 August
3. Environmental Agency (2015a) What's in your backyard. Online. http://apps.environment-agency.gov.uk/wiyby/default.aspx
4. Dhonau, M. and Rose, C. (2015) Homeowners Guide to Flood Resilence. Online. www.knowyourfloodrisk.co.uk/sites/default/files/Flood Guide_ForHomeowners.pdf
5. Public Health England (2015) Flooding: Advice for the public. Online. www.gov.uk/government/uploads/system/uploads/attachment_data/file/401980/flood_leaflet_2015_final.pdf
6. Blue Pages (2015). Online. www.bluepages.org.uk/
7. Meteorological Office (2015) Heat and sun. Online www.metoffice.gov.uk/guide/weather/severe-weather-advice-heat
8. National Health service (2015) Online. www.nhs.uk/Livewell/Summerhealth/Pages/Heatwaveredalert.aspx
9. Barford, V. (2013) 10 ways the UK is ill-prepared for a heatwave, BBC News Magazine, 18 July. Online. www.bbc.co.uk/news/magazine-23341698
10. University of West of England (2015) Drought Risk and You (DRY). Online. www1.uwe.ac.uk/et/gem/research/dry/projectcontext.aspx

11. Living with a Changing Coast (2015) Online. www.licco.eu/
12. Living with a Changing Coast (2015) Online. www.licco.eu/
13. Spanger-Siegfried, S., Fitzpatrick, M. and Dahl, K. (2014) *Encroaching Tides: How sea level rise and tidal flooding threaten US East and Gulf Coast communities over the next 30 years*, Union of Concerned Scientists
14. Sheppard, S. (2012) *Visualising Climate Change: A guide to visual communication of climate change and developing local solutions*, Earthscan/Routledge
15. Environment Agency/DEFRA (2015b) Online. Future Worlds. www.flickr.com/photos/environment-agency

## Chapter 9: Limiting climate change

1. Sewing up a hole or tear before it gets worse
2. UNEP (2015) Climate change. Online. www.unep.org/climatechange/mitigation
3. Randall, R. and Brown, A. (2015) *In Time for Tomorrow? The Carbon Conversations Handbook*, The Surefoot Effect
4. Soil Association (2015) Online. www.soilassociation.org/
5. Transition Chepstow (2015) Local food challenge. Online. www.transitionchepstow.org.uk/events/chepstow-food-challenge/
6. Randall, R. and Brown, A. (2015) *In Time for Tomorrow? The Carbon Conversations Handbook*, The Surefoot Effect
7. Next Green Car (2015) Online. www.nextgreencar.com/
8. Newcastle City Council (2014) Go Zero. Online. www.newcastle.gov.uk/parking-roads-and-transport/travel-planning/go-zero
9. Leonard, A. (2010) *The Story of Stuff: How our obsession with stuff is trashing the planet, our communities, and our health - and a vision for change*, Constable
10. International Tree Foundation (2015) Online. http://internationaltreefoundation.org/why-trees/

11. Carrington, D. (2015) Renewable energy outstrips coal for the first time in UK electricity mix, *The Guardian*, 24 September

## Chapter 10: Telling family stories

1. T. S. Eliot (1943) *The Four Quartets*, Faber
2. Lucas, C. (2011) The New Home Front: 1. Online. www.greenparty.org/assets/files/reports/the_new_hom e_front_FINAL.pdf
3. Astyk, S. (2008) *Depletion and Abundance: Life on the new home front*, New Society Publishers (p.22)
4. Harvey, F. (2015) Carbon emission cuts at a local level could avoid dangerous global warming, *The Guardian*, 7 July
5. Lucas, C. (2011) The New Home Front: 1. Online. www.greenparty.org/assets/files/reports/the_new_hom e_front_FINAL.pdf (p.11)
6. Astyk, S. (2008) *Depletion and Abundance: Life on the new home front*, New Society Publishers (pp.6-7)
7. Berners-Lee, M. and Clark, D. (2010) What is a carbon footprint? *The Guardian*, 4 June. Online. www.theguardian.com/blog/2010/jun/04/carbon-footprint- definition
8. Carbon Footprint (2015) Online. www.carbonfootprint.com
9. Berners-Lee, M. (2010) *How Bad are Bananas? The carbon footprint of everything*, Profile Books
10. Climate Footprint Calculator (2015) Online. www.carbonfootprint.com/calculator.aspx
11. Sheppard, S. (2012) *Visualizing Climate Change*, Earthscan/Routledge
12. Carbon Footprint (2015) Online. www.carbonfootprint.com
13. Earth Overshoot Day (2015) http://overshootday.org

14. Carbon Conversations (2015) Meetings. Online. www.carbonconversations.org/print/22

15. Randall, R. and Brown, A. (2015) *In Time for Tomorrow? The Carbon Conversations Handbook*, The Surefoot Effect.

## Chapter 11: Learning about sustainability

1.  Freire, P. (1994) *A Pedagogy of Hope*, Continuum (p.3)
2.  Ashden Awards (2015). Online. www.ashden.org/ashden_awards
3.  Ashden Awards (2015). Online. www.ashden.org/ashden_awards
4.  Food for Life (2015) Online. http://foodforlife.org.uk/schools/criteria-and-guidance
5.  Food for Life (2015) Online. http://foodforlife.org.uk/schools/criteria-and-guidance
6.  Eco-Schools (2015) Online. http://ecoschools.global/how-does-it-work/
7.  Eco-Schools (2015) Online. http://ecoschools.global/how-does-it-work/
8.  Owens, P. (2011) *Little Blue Planet: Investigating spaceship Earth*, Geographical Association
9.  Rayner, D. (2011) *Hot and Bothered? A study of climate change*, Geographical Association
10. Hicks, D. (2013) A post-carbon geography, *Teaching Geography*, 38 (3): 94-97
11. Field Studies Council (2015) Online. www.field-studies-council.org/
12. Assessment and Qualifications Alliance (AQA) Online. www.aqa.org.uk/about-us
13. Hicks, D. (2012) *Sustainable Schools, Sustainable Futures*, World Wide Fund for Nature. Online. www.teaching4abetterworld.co.uk/docs/download18.pdf
14. Hicks, D. (2014) *Educating for Hope in Troubled Times: Climate change and the transition to a post-carbon future*, Institute of Education Press

## Chapter 12: Creating low-carbon community

1. Rob Hopkins (2011) *The Transition Companion*, Green Books (p.17)
2. Sheppard, S. (2012) *Visualizing Climate Change: A guide to visual communication of climate change and developing local solutions*, Earthscan/Routledge
3. Transition Network (2015) Online. At www.transitionnetwork.org/
4. Transition Network principles (2015) Online. www.transitionnetwork.org/about/principles
5. Hopkins, Rob blog (2015) A remarkable day in Ungersheim. Online. http://transitionnetwork.org/blogs/rob-hopkins
6. Resilience Centre, The (2015) Online. At www.theresiliencecentre.co.uk
7. Hodgson, J. and Hopkins, R. (2010) *Transition in Action, Totnes and District 2030: An Energy Descent Plan*, Transition Town Totnes (p.17)
8. Hodgson, J. and Hopkins, R. (2010) *Transition in Action, Totnes and District 2030: An Energy Descent Plan*, Transition Town Totnes
9. Hodgson, J. and Hopkins, R. (2010) *Transition in Action, Totnes and District 2030: An Energy Descent Plan*, Transition Town Totnes (p.17)
10. Carnegie UK Trust (2011) Exploring Community Resilience in Times of Rapid Change. Online. At www.carnegieuktrust.org.uk/getattachment/75a9e0c4-8d75-4acb-afac-6b1cbd6f2c1e/Exploring-Community-Resilience.aspx
11. Hopkins, R. (2015) *21 Stories of Transition*, Transition Network

## Illustrations

Cover - 'Solar PV investors OVESCO Priory School'; Ashden Awards; www.ashden.org/images/2014_winners/uk/OVESCO/1.jpg; with permission

Page 5 - 'Pressure on polluters set to grow in 2016'; Global Call for Climate Action; http://tcktcktck.org/2016/01/pressure-on-polluters; Creative Commons 2008

Page 12 - 'Greenhouse gas by sector 2000'; Stuart Riley; www.stuartriley/net/Propaganda.html; Wikimedia Commons

Page 29 - 'Strip coal mining'; Stephen Codrington; https://en.wikipedia.org/wiki/File:Strip_coal_mining.jpg; Creative Commons by 2.5

Author: '200-year present' (page 43); 'Boys in Lakes' (page 49); 'Steam locomotive' (page 63); 'Rock pool' (page 110).

Page 55 - 'European wind makes strides'; Tierney Smith; http://tcktcktck.org/2016/02/european-wind-makes-strides-but-falls-down-global-leaderboard/; Creative Commons

Page 82 - 'Pelamis at EMEC'; P123; https://Commons.wikimedia.org/wiki/File:Pelamis_at_EMC.jpg; Wikimedia Commons

Page 97 - 'At this point in the meeting'; Cade Martin, Dawn Arlotta, USCDP; www.public-domain-image.com/free-images/people/at-this-point-in-the-meeting-they-were-about-to-address-two-meeting-participants; PIXNIO - free images

Page 103 - 'Denby Dale Passivhaus'; Green Building Store; www.greenbuildingstore.co.uk; with permission

Page 129 - 'Facing up to Rising Sea Levels'; Institute of Civil Engineers/Royal Institute of British Architects; info@riba.org; no reply to query

Page 142 - 'Government Incentive For Plug-In Vehicles'; https://en.wikipedia.org/wiki/Government_incentives_for_plug_in_electric_vehicles; Creative Commons 3.0

Page 153 - 'The Solar Settlement, Freiburg, Germany'; Andrew Glaser; https://en.wikipedia.org/wiki/Solar_Settlement; Creative Commons 3.0

Page 159 - 'Apollo 17 Image Of Earth From Space'; NASA; https://commons.wikimedia.org/wiki/File:Apollo_17_Image_Of_Earth_From_Space.jpeg#fil Wikimedia Commons

Page 184 - 'Four questions about climate change'; Geographical Association; *Primary Geography*, 2009; www.geography.org.uk; with permission

Page 198 - 'The global heart of Transition'; mmomaerts' blog; www.transitions.org/blog/global-heart-transition-reflections-2015-international-transition-network-conference; Creative Commons

## Twenty Best Reads

Ashden Awards (2015). www.ashden.org/ashden_awards

Berners-Lee, M. (2010) *How Bad are Bananas? The carbon footprint of everything*, Profile Books

Boyle, G. ed. (2012) *Renewable Energy: Power for a sustainable future*, 3rd edition, Oxford University Press

Carbon Footprint (2015) www.carbonfootprint.com

Department of Energy and Climate Change (2014) Climate change explained. www.gov.uk/climate-change-explained

Dhonau, M. and Rose, C. (2015) Homeowners Guide to Flood Resilence. www.knowyourfloodrisk.co.uk/sites/default/files/FloodGuide_ForHomeowners.pdf

Environmental Agency (2015) What's in your backyard. www.apps.environment- agency.gov.uk/wiyby/default.aspx

Environment Agency/DEFRA (2015) Future Worlds.
www.flickr.com/photos/environment-agency

Fossil Free UK (2015). http://gofossilfree.org/uk/

Hicks, D. (2014) *Educating for Hope in Troubled Times: Climate change and the transition to a post-carbon future*, Institute of Education Press

Hicks, D. (2012) *Sustainable Schools, Sustainable Futures*, Godalming: World Wide Fund for Nature.
www.teaching4abetterworld.co.uk/docs/download18.pdf

Hopkins, R. (2011) *The Transition Companion: Making your community more resilient in uncertain time*, Green Books

Hopkins, R. (2015) *21 Stories of Transition*, Totnes: Transition Network

Juniper, T. (2015) *What Nature Does for Britain*, Profile Books

Klein, N. (2015) *This Changes Everything: Capitalism vs the climate*, Penguin

Leonard, A. (2010) *The Story of Stuff*, London: Constable & Robinson

Macy, J. and Johnstone, C. (2012) *Active Hope: How to face the mess we're in without going crazy*, New World Library

Randall, R. and Brown, A. (2015) *In Time for Tomorrow? The Carbon Conversations Handbook*, Surefoot Effect

Wisser, W. (2009) *The Top Fifty Sustainability Books*, Cambridge University Press

WWF (2014) *Living Planet Report 2014.*
www.wwf.eu/media_centre/publications/

47791952R00130

Made in the USA
San Bernardino, CA
08 April 2017